the
family
within
your
walls

the family within your walls

Elliott D. Landau

INTERNATIONAL STANDARD BOOK NUMBER
0-88290-095-1

LIBRARY OF CONGRESS CATALOG CARD NUMBER
78-52116

Printed in the
United States of America
by

Horizon Publishers
& Distributors
P.O. Box 490
50 South 500 West
Bountiful, Utah 84010

*In Memory
of
Mary J. McAdie
1938-1975*

Preface

A good professor not only professes what is his own but he has his pulse on that which others may contribute to knowledge. Such is the case in this book.

Each of the columns contained in these pages was once printed in the *Deseret News* under the heading of my regular column, *Today's Family.*

The *Deseret News* is not responsible for anything I have said in this book. I have taken liberally from many sources. I have always given credit where it was due. Any additions to materials adapted from the ideas of others are completely my own beliefs. They represent only that and should not be construed by anyone to be either more or less than that.

I believe that parents, no matter what their social or educational stature may be, commence their married lives with an intense desire to rear fine families. Most folks do, too. The insights of those who have gone before us need to be examined in the light of our present experience. Accept truth where you find it. If what you read here has meaning for you, then use it to make your life better. Reject that which you disagree with only after you have tested the ideas thoroughly.

I am fond of quoting Count Alfred Korzybski who once said, "I say what I say I do not say what I do not say." This is my only disclaimer about what follows.

Table of Contents

Acknowledgments

To my family I am eternally indebted for life and experience. To those who have taught me and to those I may have taught, I am deeply grateful.

I need to thank the *Deseret News* who each Wednesday prints my views. Its general manager, William B. Smart, has been both friend and colleague and supporter.

Rose Mary Pedersen and her staff of the Living section of the *News* are always there to lend support.

There would be no book at all without the labors of Barbara Lapary and Jean Milligan who take what I write over a period of a year or so and put it into order with respect to relevancy and propriety. They are a brilliant team.

EDL

1

Introduction

Family Life is Worth It

Life without family is life, yes, but not the ultimate in human existence. Life in families is difficult, yet possible.

I have suggested that parents are very much the architects of the emotional aura that surrounds those within the family. Parents, that beautiful coalition of husband and wife, are the prime motivators in the constellation known as marriage and the family.

Children need to be seen as individuals who are in the process of development. They need to be considered as unfinished products. There is a story about the Sunday School teacher who asked the child: "Who made you?" And the child answered: "I don't know. I'm not finished yet."

At no point in human growth and development is all "lost." I believe that it is possible, both with and without help, for parents and children and families and married couples, who want to fight and stay together, to be able to maintain a certain degree of homogeneity and oneness should they want it enough.

Nothing can be held together that does not want to be. The drug addict can never become free of his illness if he wants to be enslaved to it. Husbands and wives who would rather separate will separate. If they would rather stay together, they will find ways and means of doing this.

Yes, family life is worth it.

2

Family, the Basic Building Block

Importance of the Family

On the eve of his ninetieth birthday historian Will Durant was quoted as saying, "The family has gone to pieces and marriage has gone, too. That is unfortunate, because there are two marvelous forms of order that can be pillars of strength in the flux of modern life. If you get rid of the state, the family can maintain order. But get rid of the family and you have nothing." (Deseret News, Nov. 4, 1975)

There are, as I have repeatedly said, problems with family life. There were in ancient times, there are now, and there always will be problems in folks living together.

But even under some of the meaner circumstances, family life is recalled with fondness. Dr. Theodore Lidz has called the family the only sensible way to organize life that has not yet been replaced with anything better.

The family imposes a discipline upon humans which is required for their mental and physical survival.

Children who do not flourish in a family environment grow to be mean and hateful. They become oblivious to law. They serve only themselves. When the family maintains reasonable order, it gives a child the strength to carry that sense of order into every facet of his life.

Every effort should be made not to acquiesce to grandiose federal notions that child-care experts or degree-carrying substitutes are in any sense a fair substitution for a good mother.

The nation's most interest-producing investment is in the home and family no matter what the cost. I propose that we pay mothers to stay home unless they can prove that only one loving person will care for their child.

The educational oligarchy of America will soon proclaim that the school is the proper place for infants since there really trained people will take care of children.

Let us not forget that long before there were psychological totems to worship there were mothers who nearly always knew what their children needed. One can read Julius Lester's, "Black Folk Tales" to feel the vibrant love and care uneducated slave women had for their families.

Most certainly there are people who are not capable of rearing children and where the children must be given substitute care. Let us also realize that better than 90 percent of the parents in this world are better for their children than all the Ph.Ds in America put together—including yours truly.

The order imposed by a family cannot be substituted for by any institution.

We should not permit the schools to rear our infants. When that day comes in any widespread sense, then we have as a nation spawned the beginning of a chaos which will make today's world seem the pillar of stability.

The Value of Family Relationships

There is no question but what the family unit, in no matter what shape, is a great teacher. A family in good order teaches order; in disorder, it teaches disorder.

It is within even the flimsy walls of today's family that morality may be taught.

I use the word "flimsy" advisedly here meaning that since the end of the agrarian American society as the prevailing way of life, there have been many intrusions on what was once the primary teaching force in a child's life.

In today's world he is taught by close neighbors, by electronic media, by a sophisticated school system, by the print media, and by the itinerant peddlers of ideas who now tour the lecture circuits and are reported upon daily in all of these media.

I have seen children from what most outside observers would call chaotic families by all ordinary standards, defend their parents with vehemence against the slings and arrows of "outsiders."

While it may be *de rigeur* to teach children of their interdependence with all of the world around, it is fundamental that they be taught an intense loyalty to their immediate family.

When the walls come tumbling down as they are wont to do in our hectic modern existence, too often there is no other place to turn than the family. Wherever the prevailing ethic seeks to diminish the prime importance of family and replace it with any other allegiance, the cause of true humanism and justice is thwarted.

It has been said in ancient scriptures that there are three partners in any man: God, his father, and his mother. The nourishment a child derives from parents who love him is incomparable.

I recently overheard two adolescents talking to one another. One of them had just suffered the death of both parents in an airplane crash. The other had both parents somewhere in the world, yet those parents for whatever reasons were unable to care for their child.

The latter child said, "You are still more fortunate than I. Your folks loved you, but they died. Mine have not died but don't love me enough to have me live with them."

Similarly, the old adage that says, "A little hurt from one of your kin is worse than a big hurt from a stranger," means that the greatest source of comfort comes from a family that loves. When one of your family is cruel and unthinking, it cuts deeper than any slur from a friend or teacher.

Our intrafamilial relationships are so meaningful in our total emotional lives that working to make these as perfect as possible is a task without parallel and worthy of a lifetime of effort.

Even those who run away from home, ostensibly to escape the tyranny of the family, soon learn that the hurt of leaving family ties is greater than hunger, disease and affectionate accomplices.

If we get rid of the family, we will not replace it with anything else but feigned camaraderie, which too often pales when the chips are down.

Communes Functioning as Families

Some years ago, a good friend of mine was studying communes in the USA.

Wherever he went, he found small pockets of experimental communal living, some with sexual permissiveness, few without.

But what really surprised him was that when he asked an entire group to pose for a picture, they gathered into biological families.

In spite of their way of life, instinctively, they functioned as a family.

"Functioning as families" is the only way civilization will perpetuate itself. The advancement and enhancement of our culture is dependent upon our ability to produce and prepare future generations to perform as families.

In the past, there were a great many means of support for the family carrying out its role as perpetuator.

Today, the concept of family has been undermined from many societal anchors.

Theoretically speaking, this wouldn't be so bad if anyone were able to suggest a viable alternative.

There are millions of normal families in this nation. It is shameful that only those forces which find fault with the family get heard.

Family living in a world where technological advances separate families, where child-rearing practices de-emphasize the traditional hierarchical model of family life, and where permissive liberation movements erode once time-honored family practices, is never easy.

True, the family is not a finished product. No wedding picture or announcement makes a family. No ceremony automatically creates a healthy family atmosphere.

All families have much to learn. But this does not imply that the family is a failure. It is a process, subject to study and thought.

And in the marketplace of ideas, the advocates of strong families will win, because they have civilization and cultural advancement at the root of their movement.

3

Institutionalized Care of Infants

Family Care Produces Better Children

Not too many years ago someone said that if nature had intended man to fly, it would have made him with wings.

Today we reflect upon this type of thinking and smirk.

Dr. Herbert Ratner of the Oak Park, Illinois Public Health Department recently made a similar statement about institutionalized care of children.

The only difference is that when Ratner speaks of the family and says, "If nature had intended for children to be raised in groups, they would have come in litters," he will not be put to shame in the years to come.

The institutionalized care of infants practiced by any society is counter to the will of nature. This does not mean that it cannot be, nor that it will not be done.

It does mean that man was designed to be brought up with a very special one-to-one relationship with the older generation. Anything less than this, outside of the family matrix, is certain to produce hostile, inhumane and agressive children.

Even in a family, except where there are twins, the ages of children are staggered. Thus the family is permitted by nature to give different intensities of attention to children.

The newborn can get very little care between feedings without doing it any harm, if it so happens that there is a 1-1/2-year-old child just ahead. The toddler needs more care, more watching, more human interaction, and he usually gets it because mother is able to give it to him.

The generalization of human relationships is the rule in an institution. The individualization of human relationships is the rule in families.

I know of no system in which institutional care produces better children than family care. The advocacy of state, federal or even private institutional means of rearing children is a deceptive, even cruel attempt to destroy the fullest flowering of human personality.

Even in Israel where institutional rearing of children is practiced by a tiny fraction of the population it is often emotionally unsatisfying to adults. During a visit there recently, I personally met women and men who were leaving the kibbutz rather than have the child-rearing function taken from them.

When children are grouped by age as they must be to facilitate management, in any institution caring for more than six children, an unnecessary and unhealthy child rivalry is automatically created.

While my objections to institutionalized rearing has dealt mainly with preschoolers, I reserve my most livid scorn for those who think that infants fare any better.

The history of the race proclaims the fundamental importance of infant rearing by one's immediate family or reasonable substitutes.

Parental Care is Superior

Dr. Amitai Etzione has been quoted as saying: "People no longer discharge their duty to bring up young children. There are 10 million children in the United States now who have either one or no parent. I foresee a great increase in children with character defects."

A few years ago I went out on a limb and stated that even bad families are better than good institutions for children. I still maintain that most parents are better than they think they are.

A curious mixture of modern psychology, media exposure and the movement towards liberation of both sexes has served to convince too many that they are unworthy to rear children.

This becomes especially evident to the average mother or father when they discover in themselves the seeds of envy, contempt and even hatred towards their children.

Dr. Howard Lane once said, "A certain amount of fleas is good for a dog cause it takes his mind off being a dog."

Similarly, it is inevitable and normal that parents will suffer blows to ego, happiness and well-being in the process of shaping a family.

A certain amount of frustration is normal and healthy as children are reared, because if they are to grow as reasonably fully-functioning, self-actualizing humans, they must often come into sharp conflict with their parents.

I think liberation movements have too often become beautiful cop-out avenues. I have seen it many times.

The young mother or dad finds a rather continual frustration at home with a family, where dreams of culture, worldliness and the total development of personality are bogged down in a "bucket of diapers and a barrel of bills."

With the exception of severely emotionally disturbed parents, I stoutly maintain that no woman (even one who got A grades in child-development courses) in the neighborhood nursery school (ones especially for 2-4 year olds) will be a match for even a somewhat-plagued mother, who at least sporadically enjoys her children.

Before I am attacked in the streets, let me quote Count Alfred Korzybski who once said, "I say what I say, I do not say what I do not say."

I did not say there should be an abolition of nursery schools. I did not say that there are no competent, even loving women and men who direct and teach in nursery schools. I said what I said and only what I said.

Particularly in the first three years of life, parents owe their children undivided love and concern. There is little work, except at the most advanced level of university study, that is as intellectually demanding as parenting.

No one molds character as does the parent who cares enough and loves enough to study seriously his (or her) human relationships at home.

Only dire necessity should push parents into substituting any kind of care for their own. That kind of trade-off never has been or will be worth it.

Early Child Care

What happens to a child before the age of three is crucial.

While a child may not be foredoomed by negative events prior this age, whether or not he receives attention and love is of great consequence.

A researcher, Harold Skeels, studied 13 mentally retarded children under the age of three who had average IQs of 64 and who were transferred from an orphanage, where they only received minimum care, to an institution for the mentally retarded.

Here they were loved, coddled and played with by the women inmates. This went on for an average of four years when all of the children were returned to the orphanage or adopted.

Skeels then traced these children some 23 years later and discovered these startling things:

All had finished high school and were self-supporting. Four had one or more years of college. One had a BA degree. Eleven were married. Nine of the eleven had a total of 28 children.

Thirteen other children with slightly higher IQs who had never left the orphange, were also followed up as adults. (The full results of this study are available. Consult "Adult status of children with contrasting life experiences," Monograph of the Society for Research in Child Development, 31, No. 3, Serial No. 105, 1966.)

Here are the contrasting results: One had died in adolescence, four were still in institutions, one was in a mental hospital and three were in institutions for the mentally retarded. A median of less than third grade was completed.

Those working, with one exception, were doing menial work. One subject was married and had a retarded child.

The major differences in the experience of these two groups were the attention, affection, and gifts bestowed upon them by female inmates of an institution for the mentally retarded!

The children in the institution for orphans lost 26.2 IQ points in two years, as compared with a gain of 28.5 for the children cared for by women inmates.

Thus early child care for children whether it be by massive means such as on the federal level or by one person with one child privately, must include a great deal of handling, fondling, talking to, hugging, playing, etc., by the persons who give the care.

Mere custodial attention is ruinous. In any child-care plans, it isn't so much the number of children cared for, but rather the quality of care provided, that is important.

With pretoddlers, any more than four or five children to one adult will almost certainly eliminate the attention just described.

Parental Concern for Their Young

F. Fremont-Smith once said, "What is the most humanly significant biological denominator common to all human beings and to all human groups? It occurred to me that this might be the concern of parents for their very young. This parental concern has a long biological heritage and is absolutely essential for survival of most species."

(This comment was made in 1960 by Fremont-Smith and is found in the volume, "The Central Nervous System and Behavior," edited by M.A.B. Brazier in the "Transactions of the Third Conference" of the Josiah Macy, Jr. Foundation.)

One of the major differences between Homo sapiens and all other groups is the long state of dependence of the children on the parents.

In most mammals the period of infant dependency is a matter of months...a year in monkeys, several years in apes, but at least six to eight years in humans.

Of all the species on the earth, man has the slowest rate of growth. For example, human brains at birth are but a quarter of the size they will be finally. By the age of six a brain has reached 9 percent of its final weight, but it takes until age twenty or thereabouts for it to stop growing.

The human infant at birth is far more helpless than nearly any other mammal. It is clear to biologists that man's prolonged helplessness is the very thing which necessitates his development in a family in which both mother and father are vitally concerned.

To the extent that this concern is missing, diminished or abbreviated in significant ways, especially in early childhood, there will be severe trauma in the human being thus offended.

A more detailed study of this may be found in Peter Rowland's "Children Apart" (New York: Pantheon Books, 1973).

For many reasons the long-term association of human infants with their parents makes for a reciprocal social-relationship situation—even an intensely emotional relationship. In females it was once called "maternal instinct." The term is virtually discarded now and has been replaced with an equally powerful one, "mutual stimulation."

This helps to explain how some mothers can kill their children (the infanticide rate is soaring in Japan), others really not like them very much, and yet still others be willing to lay down their lives for their children.

If mother receives a great deal of satisfaction from nurturing her child, this wonderful feeling of joy and comfort is transmitted to the child, who in turn reflects it in his behavior.

The social bond between parents and children, especially between mothers and their children is, at first, greatly enhanced or retarded by the stimulation received during the nursing period.

There is much literature about the biochemical affects of nursing and its attendant psychological effects.

In general, the evidence is strong that in every facet of mother-child relationships, breast-feeding attitudes and success correlate highly with success in child rearing.

If you would like to pursue this further, consult "Parenthood: Its Psychology and Psychopathology" edited by Anthony and Benedek (Boston: Little-Brown, 1970).

Harlow's Monkeys— A Lesson in Love

Results of research on primates seem to have some pretty definite implications for our knowledge of human behavior.

However, the word implications does not mean that if a certain fact is true about monkeys that, *ipso facto,* it is true about humans.

Dr. Harry Harlow has done 40 years of spectacular work with monkeys. In his years of research on the affectional love systems demonstrated in monkeys, which may also be valid for humans, he has identified five types of love.

These are maternal (the love of mother for child); infant (the love for infants); peer (the love of children for children); heterosexual (the love that exists between persons of opposite sexes); and parental (the love of fathers for children).

Harlow, in his lecture entitled, "Agression and Love" delivered at the New York Academy of Medicine, October 31, 1975, emphasized the importance of the two systems of maternal and peer love in teaching a child control of those "innate learned emotions, hostility and aggression, which are not apparent at birth but mature late in the mother-infant system of love."

One of Harlow's major findings, which I think makes sense, is that the consequence of being brought up without a rich exposure (in his experiments monkeys grew up without any contact at all from mothers or peers) to maternal or peer love, is the creation of a suicidal animal who, once becoming a mother herself, either ignores her own offspring or violently abuses them.

In fact, the cruelty of these motherless mothers was so horrendous that even the staunchest of Harlow's graduate students were unable to stomach what they say. These motherless mothers crushed the skulls of their little ones and rubbed off their faces by scraping their heads along the concrete floor.

The discovery that these infants were almost perpetually loyal to their vicious mothers is nothing short of amazing.

In fact, if the babies were able to survive the onslaught of their mothers they, through their persistence and loyalty, succeeded in inducing their mothers to succumb to their continual efforts to love and nuzzle them. In other words the infants became therapists for their own mothers.

What does this all add up to?

First, I am willing to hazard the guess that humans, like monkeys, need early loving and continual peer interaction in order to grow up sane.

Second, human children are amazingly resilient, much as baby monkeys aren't.

Third, children have a wit and wisdom that is therapeutic to adults who are ill.

Finally, if primates and humans are not sufficiently loved in their youth, they run the danger of being raised to be haters.

The clue for all of us: Whatever care adults give children must be saturated with warm, physical affection lest abnormal children be the product.

Working Mothers

The topic of working mothers is always a difficult one to tackle. This is especially true where there is an inflated economy and when it is nearly impossible to make ends meet, no matter how many work in the family.

What happens to children when both parents work full-time? I know of no evidence that contradicts the following:

Other things being equal, there is no concern so deep, so genuine, so at times even overly-involved (this to the detriment of the child) than that of concerned parents.

There is no one other than grandparents, close relatives or friends who really can care, or even should care about the guidance of children who are not their own.

This may sound crass at first. But let's face it—when the chips are down, it is only the parent who cares enough to charge into the school, the dentist's office or into the little league director to fight for the welfare of a child.

On rare occasions there are other interested parties who will go to bat for your child's welfare.

But these people usually have their own families, their own problems, and they will run with the ball just so far. Then they'll turn around and slip you, the parent, a lateral pass.

There is always someone who will write to me or protest that I have a dim view of humans. So be it. I know that even the finest professionals can go just so far, and then they turn to the next case, as well they must.

I had a deaf aunt who was the bravest soul in all the world. Her child is today confined to an institution for the unmanageable mentally retarded because of her deafness and asocial behavior.

Until the day my aunt died, she maintained that if only people understood Sandy they would realize that she could be managed.

And she was right. My Aunt Lizzy taught that child to sew, to cook, to clean herself, her room. She "managed" her because she loved her with a ferocity that no childcare expert in any setting could be expected to evince.

I don't think parents working will ruin children or marriages. But I think work should be delayed until the children are at least school age whenever possible.

If you want your child's intellect and heart to flourish (as opposed to simply grow), no one can encourage the project like you, the parent.

It takes two people to create a fully-functioning child. No matter how efficient, carefully staffed or technically trained an institution's faculty may be, it can do little more than provide the trappings of care.

The irrevocable commitment to the deep-down welfare of the child in every significant aspect is reserved for the parents.

Children Alone

One of the most terrifying experiences a young child may be faced with is the separation from those he loves. Even temporary separation has the seeds of trauma to the child's emotional development in it.

Separation due to illness and separation due to divorce or parental dissolution of normal living arrangements are topics that have intrigued me for nearly a quarter of a century.

The "hard" research data is not easily available, but hundreds of anectdotal records attest to the severe trauma young children experience in even brief separation.

My conclusions are simply this: until the age of five I would be very wary of hospitalizing a child unless it is an acute emergency or unless the hospital makes specific provisions for parents to sleep near their child.

Under the age of three I would not allow hospitalization even overnight unless the parent could be there every second of the time.

Unfortunately, too many hospitals in the materially-developed world are not aware of the intense pain and after-effects of even brief separation.

Under the age of three and including the third year, no amount of adult explanations are completely comprehensible to the child who must go into strange surroundings for as little as an overnight stay.

In fact, these hospitals will assure parents that the nursing staff are excellent. And they usually are. But that is not the issue.

Nursing care, at best, cannot involve sufficient affection and cuddling.

Children under three need the warmth and concern of folks who consider them integral to their lives as a family. As wonderful as nurses are, they do have many children to care for and they are not, after all, the parents.

In the matter of divorce or separation, my sources indicate that where a marriage can be saved "for the sake of the children" (and it is true that this is rapidly becoming an unfashionable phrase) it ought to be.

There are circumstances which indicate that divorce is the only road open. But when a couple decides to stay together for the sake of the children, they show they can manage their lives within the context of their present unhappiness.

It is a general rule that the older children are the easier it is for them to make sense of the parents' decision to divorce. Under the age of eight or thereabouts, children, regardless of cause, feel abandoned and guilty when their parents split.

They cannot comprehend the intricacies of adult decisions. And they certainly do not understand how at-home difficulties necessitate separation since they have plenty of troubles at home, and they can't split when they please.

Should the decision to break up a marriage be irrevocable it is wise to decide upon telling the children the truth, except where that truth will seriously lay the blame for the split upon one or the other of the parents.

Needless to say, once the separation is in effect neither spouse must ever convey to the child his feelings of hatred or disgust for the other.

This forces the child to side with someone and that someone tends to be the one he is living with. Therefore, there has been a deception that the child knows, and this can affect his life for years to come.

The most fearful dream of humans is to be left alone in the dark and dreary world unloved, unwanted by those closest to us. When children are separated from their parents, for whatever reason, they dwell with the feelings of unwantedness which are rarely easily conquered.

Above all else in the world children need to be needed and loved. Anyone who communicates otherwise hurts the child's image of himself.

A wounded self-image is not subject to the simplicity of flat tire repairs. There is little human patchwork which "takes" for very long.

An Israeli Kibbutz

Jordan Valley, Israel—I'm writing this article sitting in a one-room cottage heated only by a small kerosene lamp.

There are three crude cots in my 20' by 14' abode and a room full of 20-year-olds next door practicing their recorders.

The shower I just took was in a very rough sort of shower room as unprivate as could be (well, there was a door!). It's shared by others, as is everything else on this Israeli Kibbutz called Mesillot.

This lush valley is about 50 miles north of Jerusalem and 15 miles south of the Sea of Galilee and is located 600 feet below sea level at the eastern tip of the Jezreel Valley, known to many as the Valley of Armageddon.

Kibbutz Mesillot started in 1935 when it was conceived as a land "Haartzi Kibbutz" or "collective," by Jews from Eastern Europe who were members of the Mapan (United Labor Party).

It was their intention then, as it is now, to found totally non-religious, Jewish collectives. Its present secretary is Shlomo Frank, my host.

He is the father of three children, about 63 years old, and has been a member of this kibbutz for over 40 years.

Sitting in his very modest home is a unique experience. There is a total absence of luxury.

In fact, throughout my visits in so many homes here the most obvious discovery is that nearly everyone lives in an austerity which is sufficient to bring a slight flush of embarrassment to a middle-class American.

Except for a very few, there are no automobiles, no dish-washers, tubs, kitchens.

It is an armed society where every family is certain to find both boys and girls in the army by the age of 18.

On every bus, in every street, at every corner, every school, and in Kibbutz Mesillot there are armed guards, young and old, on duty.

As a guest of the Israeli government I came to Israel for the specific purpose of observing child care in the kibbutz, in school, and at home.

My next article will deal with this subject.

Child Care on the Kibbutz

Jordan Valley, Israel—There are several thousand women in Israel who live on kibbutzim and who have their children raised from birth by others in their community.

Dr. Mordecai Kaffman and I sat talking about this in his office in Tel Aviv. He is presently the medical director, Kibbutz Child and Family Clinic, in this great city.

This is how he describes the difference between the traditional way of family functioning and kibbutz child-rearing:

"In most of the communal settlements, children live in separate houses. Each constitutes a complete functional unit geared to the rearing and comprehensive needs of a small group of children of the same age who live with several caretakers.

"The caretakers assume the many functions ordinarily performed by parents. After the first six months of life, they have almost complete responsibility for every aspect of child-rearing."

The original motivation for the development of this type of child-rearing was two-fold.

One, to allow pioneer parents in the early days of the land of Palestine (now Israel since 1948) to concentrate on their farm labors so that the land could blossom like a rose.

In order to accomplish this major land revolution it was urgent that parents be able to work a full day unfettered with the complications of family life.

Fifty or sixty years ago the theorists about kibbutz development also worked on the assumption that there must be a way to halt the multigenerational neurosis characteristic of modern society.

And that constitutes the second reason for the development of this type of child-rearing.

These early pioneers genuinely believed that the kibbutz technique of replacing the parent with a person not emotionally bound to the child through actual lineage would isolate the neuroses of mothers and fathers and avoid the neurotic contamination of the second generation.

It was thought then that the kibbutz could eliminate emotional conflict between parents and children by encouraging permissive child-rearing techniques, avoiding punishment and acknowledging respect for the child's sense of autonomy.

Obviously, the dreamy ideals the early band of pioneers had about child-rearing were doomed to failure. What is especially peculiar to me is that it has persisted for all of these decades with very little substantive change.

Quite clearly there is no way to avoid parent-child conflict in any system—except perhaps where children are so completely isolated from their parents that there is no chance of conflict.

Since the Israelis have always been basically family-oriented this extreme never occurred.

At any rate, here is Dr. Kaffman's comment as it appears in his famous article entitled, "Family Conflict in the Psychopathology of the Kibbutz Child," which appeared first as an address to the 7th Congress of the International Association for Child Psychiatry and Allied Professions, Jerusalem, August, 1970

"Notwithstanding all these hope and motives, the problem of multigenerational neurosis in due course made its appearance in the kibbutz system of living.

"Kibbutz theoreticians were forced to recognize that emotional conflict is an inevitable component of life, present in both normal and abnormal development."

Stages of Kibbutz Child Development

Jordan Valley, Israel—All of the normal sounds are there as you walk by the tiny cribs, four to a room.

There are infants, diapers, crying—but no mothers in sight.

This is Kibbutz Mesillot in Israel, where the community has agreed to completely separate child-rearing from the normal mother-father relationship, as is known in most of Israel and as it is in the USA.

From the moment a baby is born in Mesillot he is in the care of a metapelet (child-care person). During the first year of life, mother feeds the baby once a day and the rest of the time, he is fed and cared for by a system of assistants.

During the various stages of early life the child moves from one children's house to another with the metapelet always going along. Generally there are six children, and no more, to one metapelet and one assistant helper.

At Mesillot the children will move to four houses from birth through the age of twelve.

During the evening the adult-to-child ratio changes drastically, with only three women taking care of about a hundred children.

This is accomplished through an intercommunication system, which links every room in the children's house with a central control. If a baby gets up, cries or needs help, his sounds are heard and a child-care helper comes to take care of him.

At the age of 14 children are boarded at the same kibbutz as their parents. However, they are assigned a room with an age-mate of the same sex in a dormitory-like building.

They live this way, seeing their parents whenever they choose, or when they get the chance.

At 18 all boys and girls go into the Israeli army, regardless of sex or physical condition. At 20, the girls return; the boys, at 21. (From that time on everyone is in the reserve up to age 55.)

The boys and girls then will work for three years for the kibbutz for room and board and about $50 per month.

Should some university accept a boy at the age of 24 (23 for girls), he applies to the kibbutz for a study grant. He will be totally supported at any university for as long as his education takes.

As the Kibbutznik (a child who has grown up in a kibbutz) nears the end of his college career he will usually marry a girl from a different kibbutz, since marrying from the commune in which he was raised is taboo.

After all, since birth the boys and girls have grown up as brothers and sisters.

The Results of Kibbutz Child Raising

Jordan Valley, Israel—Is the kibbutz-reared child "normal?"

Are parents happy being separated from their children?

These are the questions most frequently asked about this type of child-care.

Implied in the kibbutz experiment is the notion that perhaps the family is not as vital to child-rearing as we thought.

Indeed, there are those who call for the end of the nuclear family and who point to Israel as the prime example of how successfully children may be reared without their parents.

It would be a total misunderstanding of the kibbutz to infer that the family is not an integral part of the plan. Communal living in the Israeli kibbutz is very family oriented. The feeling of family is very strong.

Nonetheless, children in many kibbutzim are reared almost entirely by others than the parents, except for the few hours per day they spend at home.

My informant, Dr. Mordecai Kaffman, told me that his studies indicate he has failed to uncover any clinical entity recognizable as a specific or prevalent emotional disturbance of kibbutz children.

He presently is medical director of the Kibbutz Child and Family Clinic in Tel Aviv.

Others, like Bruno Bettleheim do not agree. (Read his "Children of the Dream," New York: Macmillan Co., 1969.)

One of the more competent studies of the kibbutz child is Melford Spiro's "Children of the Kibbutz" (Cambridge: Harvard University Press, 1958).

My personal observations of this unique system of child-rearing buttress Kaffman's theory.

For Israel's particular dilemma where independent, peer-oriented, tough men need to be bred to learn to survive, it appears to be an excellent vehicle for producing children who will be totally for the cause.

In fact, I am told that a disproportionate share of the higher military officers come from the kibbutz.

It's apparent that children reared this way are more attached to country and peer group than home and family, even though they are never told they do not have a family or that their family is less important than their peers.

I was impressed with every aspect of the system, although I believe there is no alternative to the traditional family child-rearing which is practiced in 97 percent of Israel, even as it is in the United States.

But if massive child-care is the order of the day, then it is done superbly by the Israelis.

Loving, Communicating and Disciplining

4

Love and the First Three Years of Life

The awesome importance of a great deal of adult attention, affection and self-discipline given to children in the first three to four years of life is nowhere better illustrated than in the report by Harold Skeels concerning two groups of mentally-retarded children from an orphanage. One of the groups was transferred for approximately four years to an institution for the mentally retarded where women inmates loved and played with them. That group was later shown to have achieved far greater success in meeting the challenges of normal living than the other group.

The major difference in the experience of these two groups of children was the affection bestowed upon them by inmates of a mental institution.

Surely those of you who think you are incompetent mothers should feel at least as able as inmates of a mental hospital?

There is abundant evidence that as Bettleheim once said, "Never again in your life will you be so important to a human being."

He meant, of course, that in the earliest years of a child's life the major influence in his life is not food, riches or toys. It is the pure and unadulterated love, fondling and affection of the adults who live around him.

The research of Marcelle Geber in a 1958 report in the "Journal of Social Psychology" says that a study of 300 East African babies showed a clear superiority over Western European or American children in that at 7 weeks they were sitting up unaided, watching themselves in a mirror; at seven months they were walking to a box and looking inside for toys. These children receive even more parental attention than European and American infants.

The same accomplishments occur in our children at about 24 weeks and 15 months respectively.

I have before talked about everyone's intense wish for the secret formula that will guarantee fine children.

If anything approaches it, I believe it is the notion that, other things being equal, a normal mother and father can give massive doses of affection to their children as no one else can.

I know that early childhood love far outweighs the importance of nutrition in the total development of the competent, well-adjusted child. In no sense does this mean that discipline, both from parents and from the child himself, is not a vital component.

The younger a child is the less he needs to be disciplined. Correction by adults of children's behavior needs always to be meted out in response to what it is clear the child can understand.

Telling a two-year-old to be quiet when everyone else is noisy represents an unfair demand.

Slapping, harsh talk and similar adult remedies applied before the child is really able to comprehend the meaning of this type of behavior represents only a loss of affection to the child at a time when he needs approval and adult love.

Love Defined

Parents should give their children love. This is the one indispensable requirement for nourishing a child so that he will grow up to be good and loving himself.

But what does "love" mean in behavioral terms? What do you do when you love a child?

In Ray Bradbury's science-fiction story, *"I Sing the Body Electric"* (Bantam Books, 1969), the mechanical surrogate mother-grandmother talks to the family:

"Everything you ever say, everything you ever do, I'll keep, put away, treasure...I shall recall what you forgot. Love is the ability of someone to give us back to us."

A parent who loves does not take from children. He helps the child to accept himself with delight.

A parent who loves is compassionate. He is not merely a spectator in the life of the child nor a recorder merely indexing events. Compassion is a strength of personality.

"It is a means of entering into an emotional fellowship," says psychologist Arthur Jersild.

A compassionate parent understands the passions of others. He instinctively feels what his children are feeling, and he is able to translate that feeling for them and with them.

In that sense, he is giving the child back to himself.

There is a real difference between sympathy and compassion.

In a sense, sympathy implies feeling the same as another does and does not necessarily mean wishing to alleviate the pain or hurt.

Compassion is a higher order of sympathy. Compassion is love because it seeks to do more than empathize. It is a more active kind of behavior.

Perhaps this is niggling over meaning. Whatever love may or may not be, one thing is certain. Kids know instinctively whether it is there or not.

When they can't sense it, their lives are doomed to disorder. Knowing that it is present in the fullest degree gives them a deep feeling of belonging somewhere.

How to Show Your Child You Love Him

Everyone, it seems, tell folks they ought to love their children. Most people think they do. And I believe them.

Others, especially when there is trouble aplenty, say that they love their children and cannot understand what went wrong.

Still others say they think they love their children. After all, they hug them, kiss them and play with them.

But what should you *really* do when you love your children?

First, be cheerful, even though cheerfulness may not be returned. Too many parents expect something in return from their children.

This sounds extreme. That is, we give, give, give, and should we not expect something back? Of course we should, and we often do receive it. But for many years, it is very difficult for children to voice their love, and still more difficult to show it.

Studies indicate that only highly immature parents expect tit for tat with regard to love and affection. Indeed, folks who abuse a child often say that he did not return their affection so they became angry with the ungrateful youngster.

Showing love does not mean that you must accept every behavior of the child. Not at all. But when upset with a youngster, try to avoid describing his behavior. At least, do it objectively.

When you begin to describe the child's mean behavior, you assume that he doesn't know what he did. This is demeaning. Of course he knows.

Describe your feelings about his behavior. He needs to know very much that you are personally hurt.

The silent treatment isn't any better for children than it is for adults. Anger towards a child is legitimate, but it must not linger on for days.

Some folks use the "treatment" cruelly. Feelings of rejection and guilt aren't bad for a child as long as they get some relief. But long and interminable lengths of silence and anger show a child that you do not love him.

Guilt, anger and rejection are healthy, but they must not go unrelieved.

Consider, too, that the way you show your anger to your children sets a pattern for them. In other words, making up is very important. It's also fun.

Finally, showing love means doing things with a child. If anything, modern America does too much for children, too little with them.

It isn't wrong for a wife to ask a husband to take the children along, if at all possible. When going along with parents isn't accidental, but deliberate and planned, then children really begin to feel their parents' love.

Parents would be wise to note the kind of behavior they have been exhibiting in the areas listed above, and how they can improve. Even write it out.

Remember, every child needs to be loved. Loving is lots more than just hugging and kissing.

But huggin' and kissin' help.

Mirroring Feelings—A Key to Better Discipline

Every person needs to share thoughts and feelings with someone who really understands—with someone who will accept his feelings without always trying to change them.

Parents who realize this have in their possession one of the keys to better discipline. Children have a feeling of deep relief when they know they can be freely and honestly heard, when what they believe and what they understand is accepted as being their valid feelings.

When parents try to feel what a troubled child is feeling, when they are able to reflect or mirror his feelings, they let him know of their concern and sympathy. This act alone is frequently sufficient to make the child sense there is somebody who knows and understands.

It is often the verbal remarks parents make that transmit a message of concern or unconcern.

For example, when two children are battling about who should play in what part of the room, it might be sufficient for a mother to say: "You don't want your sister near you just now, I know. Maybe we can get her interested in something else and then you can play alone for a while."

This approach is far superior to a mother entering a room and saying: "You're driving me crazy! You two are always fighting. Get out of the room."

Parents are always in a position of suggesting things for children to do. Rather than enter into a pitched battle about a suggestion that has been obviously rejected by the child, it is possible to say something like this: "You don't like my suggestion. I can see that." Then discuss the alternatives with the child.

A great many things that parents say to their children convey the message that the parents are disgusted and shocked by the children's attitudes or behavior.

When children discover that parents consider them to be weird and different, they tend to play up their weirdness and differences...and right to the hilt!

The technique of reflecting their inner feelings and ideas is one way to express to them that you understand how they may be feeling, even though you are not siding with their ideas.

When parents do not reject out of hand their thoughts and feelings, the children will be likely to come to a more rational decision about how they should behave.

Discipline Through Anger

Children aren't plow mules. I hear tell that to make a mule do what you want him to do, you have to really give him a whipping and make sure that you keep on whipping.

Too many parents believe that their children need to be whipped and spoken to angrily when it comes to disciplining them for doing wrong.

There is the general belief that the message simply has to be "imbedded" in the child.

Effective disciplining of children ought to be accomplished without anger. I can hear the retort of many now..."You mean when my child does something wrong, you want me to gently and sweetly explain to him what was wrong and let it go at that?"

In a way that is precisely what I mean, even though it seems to be anti-human and certainly anti-parent.

Let's look at it this way. The real reason we become angry with children is that we feel certain the more we show our anger, the more we will convince the child how wrong he was, how upset we are and how much he needs to change.

When we become *very* angry at a child—perhaps angry enough to hit him and sometimes hurt him, then we feel that this has been a firm, valuable and visible demonstration so that the child will never forget what happened.

Yet it is a certainty that the very children who need the most disciplining are those who have repeated over and over again a wrong act. The loss of parental emotional control does not in any way guarantee that the behavior will never be demonstrated again.

The crux of the entire matter is what is known as instant repay. I sometimes call it the "slot machine syndrome" in rearing children.

The "slot machine syndrome" says this: If I hit the right combination (anger, fury, resentment and disappointment) then I am sure to have a payoff from a child and that payoff will result in an instant jackpot.

What's the jackpot?

Of course, the jackpot is permanently changed behavior, or at least the contriteness of the child to the degree that submissiveness and remorse will make it certain that the kind of behavior we just disciplined will never happen again.

However, changing children's behavior rarely occurs in the moment of a dramatic, violent and traumatic disciplinary measure.

The effects of parental guidance are very rarely immediate. In fact, it's one of the areas in which parents need to have a great deal of faith—faith in the belief that when we talk resolutely, yet quietly to a child, he understands the gravity of our intentions and the nature of his transgression. All parents need to hope that time will have its effects.

For example, let us imagine that an eight-year-old has just run his bicycle straight through a pile of bicycles that were left standing outside of a neighbor's house.

This wanton and destructive act is something that appalls the neighbors who report the incident directly to the offender's mother. An immediate response would be to go out and wallop the daylights out of this bad boy.

I'm suggesting that a severe talk, while perhaps not yielding immediate results, will have its desired effect. The only trouble is, most parents imagine that if they do not apply severe controls, which are the result of intense anger, the child's misbehavior will undoubtedly lead to delinquency.

Indeed, it isn't at all unusual to hear parents say, "If I don't nip it in the bud now, it's certain to blossom later."

Be assured that delinquency does not occur because children are given a single instance of parental moderation. Most delinquency is the result of a series of misunderstandings and poor human relationships at home that have persisted for a long period of time.

Indeed, it is not at all unusual to find perpetual delinquents stating that they have always suffered physical violence and anger from the folks they grew up with at home.

The demon bike-crasher is most unlikely to become the hard-core juvenile delinquent unless special conditions co-exist with the anger of his parents.

Far better for parents to quietly take the child inside the house and very deliberately and emphatically discuss their fears about his misbehavior, their apprehensions about the possibility of his hurting others and about the callousness of the bicycle-crashing act.

It is then and only then that we can expect the seriousness of his transgression to dawn and to more likely put an end to that kind of behavior.

Spanking

Brigham Young gave some sage counsel regarding spanking children.

I know of no more cogent or understandable and psychologically-sound advice than what was recorded in his "Journal of Discourses" (Vol. 10, pp. 360-361). He said, "Kind words and loving actions towards children will subdue their uneducated natures a great deal better than the rod, or, in other words, than physical punishment. Although it is written that, 'The rod and reproof give wisdom; but a child left to himself bringeth his mother to shame,' and, 'he that spareth the rod hateth his son; but he that loveth him chasteneth him betimes;' these quotations refer to wise and prudent corrections. Children who have lived in the sunbeams of parental kindness and affection, when made aware of a parent's displeasure, and receive a kind reproof from parental lips, are more thoroughly chastened, than by any physical punishment that could be applied to their persons....

"When children are reared under the rod...it not infrequently occurs, that they become so stupefied and lost to every high-toned feeling and sentiment, that though you bray them in a mortar among wheat with a pestle, yet will not their foolishness depart from them."

I have been observing children and their parents for many years.

I have observed parents who have fallen into the habit of hitting in order to speed the process of correction along. Indeed, I have often been asked if I did not believe the Biblical admonitions that Brigham Young quoted.

I have replied over and over that there are times when it is urgent and necessary to apply the rod. What Brigham Young is really talking about in this discourse is the habit we may fall into of correcting our children by the sole method of physical punishment.

The phrase "they become so stupefied and lost to every high-toned feeling and sentiment" is particularly fascinating.

It was almost as if Brigham Young knew that the children of men soon would be inundated with media which would parade before young minds and hearts thousands of hours of brutality, sadism and flagrant violations of decent human relations.

The fear today is not so much that children will, after viewing violence, go out and become violent (although the evidence is that they often do) but rather that they will become inured to "hightoned feeling." The more modern word is "callous" to brutality and deprivation.

Lest there be those who think that Brigham Young was only talking of whippings let me remind you that a good whipping on rare occasions may be in order. Rather, it is the continual meeting of children's intractability with the spat, the almost habitual use of the back of the hand rather than the "sunbeams of parental kindness and affection" that are injurious.

Physical punishment is the last act of a desperate parent. Its use means you have given in and have lost your adult standing. Hitting is child's behavior.

Besides, even in the boxing world where kindness isn't a hallmark of virtue, officials would never allow a welterweight in the ring with a heavyweight.

How often do you think a 30-pound child can take the swift, sure arm of a 110-pound adult?

The Father-Child Relationship

It is relatively easy to write that parents, particularly Dads, should be sensitive to the needs, feelings and moods of children. What one *does* about this admonition may not be as easy to explain.

The following situations should be excellent cues regarding father's at-home behaviors:

—You've been at work all day and when you get home it is a minor celebration. Your child is dying to spill all about school or whatever happened at home and agree to listen.

Do you then pick up the paper and demand not to be bothered?

How is it that you haven't ten minutes for your son when he needs to review his life, yet on Saturday you have a full five hours for golf?

These poor priorities are not unnoticed by children. Such early life experiences may not be easily verbalized by them, who are in many ways powerless to register disapproval until they get to be 14 or so. Be assured that 'benign neglect' accrues and often explodes in adolescence.

—Dinner is over and dad, addicted to any one of a hundred violent cops-and-robbers type TV programs, takes off for his den for the remainder of the evening.

Once home a father owes a reasonable share of at-home time to his children. A father hooked on TV cannot complain of a son similarly snagged.

A friend reports that his son, returning from his first semester at college, refused to join his dad in the nightly mystery TV show saying, "Dad, you just have to learn to use your time better."

—As soon as Daddy gets home a child is put to bed—even though the child has waited all day and needs this time to develop rapport with his father.

Big folks want time to themselves. A child who gets put to bed as his father appears on the scene will never remember the intimate moments they might have spent tussling or reading together just before bedtime.

Remember, adolescents seldom tune out parents who were tuned in during the first 12 or 13 years. If you don't like the investment, you should not have gambled in the first place.

Once in the game there is no better advice than to play for keeps. The day comes all too soon when children repay the investment commensurate with the quality of that expenditure.

There is no such thing as a free lunch. You can never withdraw more from a relationship with children than you have put in.

Communication

Parents can either "make or break" their children in four areas of adult behavior—communication, coping, self-reliance and self-image.

First of all, communication:

From the moment of birth to the time the child leaves home to form a new coalition with a spouse, what he hears and feels in the way of communication from his parents determines how he will respond to them, his world, himself, and to his own children.

Communication doesn't suddenly stop at 14, as some believe. Frankly, I don't think Patty Hearst suddenly stopped talking to her parents. She recently said (according to the magazine, Rolling Stone) that she became tired of the middle-class way of life and decided to reject it.

Well, if I know the "middle-class" life of families at the Hearsts' social level, it frequently includes a great deal of socialization, which excludes children in many ways.

In fact, on a much lower social scale, among affluent people, there is little time for deep parent-child communications.

Trips, vacations, business-related forays and the like preclude these parents having the time or inclination to really listen to their children's tales, much less exchange life expectancies with them.

Poor folks haven't been told to communicate; rich folks haven't the time.

Listening is a vital component of communication. Children have a great deal to say.

At three, it becomes insistent and tiresome. By four, children have pretty well learned how much their folks really care to hear about their world.

At eight, they have most effectively gauged their parents' responses and behave accordingly, until they separate from them.

It is only with a great deal of effort that a lost or lame eight years of communication can be ameliorated by parental change of habit.

It is my belief that if "the bell tolls for thee" in the matter of parent-child communication, now is the time to resolve to study yourself and your children and learn to do better.

The Talmud on Fathers, Sons and Family

From the Talmud, the Hebrew commentary on the First Five Books of the Old Testament, we hear much about the relationship between husbands, wives, fathers and sons and family. One of the stimulating activities for a family to engage in is the around-the-table interpretation of the wisdom of the ages.

Not too long ago I read this to my family: "If you teach your children in their youth, they won't have to teach you in your old age." I doubt that there is any one single interpretation of this bit of wisdom, but its depth is grist for young and old minds alike.

One listener to this adage felt that if children are taught respect and honor when young, there is less likelihood that they will, when grown, insult their parents by trying to teach them as if they were children.

Among a great many people there is a certain revulsion about didactic instruction of the young. It is odd how these very same folks who object to direct instruction of children in the ways of honesty and purity were so livid about the Watergate mess!

May I suggest that occasional family gatherings to chew upon truths are not only the province of the religionist but the duty of all men who wish to purify the American air and purge it of deceit, petty villainy and cronyism.

The Talmud says: "It is better that a child should cry than its parents." How many times I have disciplined my children with an aching heart. Yet, parents know (or should know) when to be firm and suffer the anger, tears and outrages of their children.

When the children cry because their parents have restricted their activities, there is less likelihood that the parents will cry later.

We have recently experienced our children working during the summer at some very difficult, exhausting labor. In fact, we visited our children (visibly and invisibly) to see them at their labors. And there were times when they cried about their tasks and wished to be released from the servitude.

We were rewarded when one day one of them commented upon how difficult it must be to feed, clothe, house and entertain four or five children. The worth of money and labor was very real.

One of the great sages of the Talmud, Nachman of Bratslav, said, "When a father is quick-tempered, his children are confused."

A quick-tempered father regularly loses his patience with the meanderings, munchings and misinterpretations of the young. But we need to remember that children don't have the world down pat. Often they are not sure what things mean. Being quick-tempered with children means that one regularly does not allow for youthful folly, misinterpretation and tomfoolery.

When the normal behavior of children arouses a quick temper they become confused about what the world is all about. Besides, it is also said that, "Wherever children are learning, there dwells the Divine Presence." The home is where much of the great learnings take place. One only learns well in an atmosphere of love and understanding.

This last word to all who teach children of other people. The sages have said, "About his children, every parent is blind." It is not a copout or a disgrace for parents not to believe what they hear about their children. In fact, a parent too eager to hear evil about his child is to be suspect as a fit parent.

How well I remember an uncle of mine refusing to believe a judge who committed his daughter to an institution for the severely retarded after she had acted out against the community.

To this day, some 30 years later, she still is in strict custodial care, yet her father is as blind to her maniacal temper now as he was then. If parents aren't blind in their allegiance to their children, they are remiss. Naturally, they are equally at fault if they do not eventually consider expert opinion.

How about sitting down tonight and trying this last one out on your family? "One father can support ten children but ten children cannot support one father." Have fun.

Obedience, Conscience, and Developing Character   5

Self-Understanding

Three primary goals of parents as they rear children are:
1. To help children gain a useful *self-understanding.*
2. To help children become *competent.*
3. To aid them in becoming *independent.*

Parents foster these goals through the family environment—its activities, its philosophy, its way of working.

Interestingly, the three tasks of any therapist are identical.

What has happened to people who seek psychiatric help is that, for whatever reasons, they do not feel they understand their own behaviors; they do not feel confident and fulfilled in many areas of their existence, and they are more dependent (emotionally and otherwise) than independent.

The purpose of psycho-therapy is to explore the difficulties in these domains with the explicit purpose of restoring a reasonable modicum of self-esteem to the patient.

It is often true that adult functioning problems are related to childhood family experiences.

Thus, it should be possible for parents, once alerted to their own proper roles, to set about guiding their children in each of these critical developmental areas so that they maximize their child's potential.

Helping children gain a useful self-understanding should begin as early as possible in the child's life. He ought to be challenged in a concerned and affectionate way to explore the reasons for his behavior.

Parents who do this without demanding complete explanations; parents who are willing to accept the "I don't know" reply are more likely to build into the child the self-inquiry attitude which is prerequisite to eventual self-understanding.

When parents are able to say, "Well, let's take a look at how you feel (felt) about what you said or did," they are forcing the child into examining his motivation for his behavior.

Especially during early adolescence (11-16) it is urgent that parents adopt the therapeutic stance of always helping a child analyze his behavior.

A child must also learn to evaluate his behavior against his code of conduct (learned at home, at school, on the street and in his religious activities).

A sure sign of growth toward self-understanding is when a child can step back enough to label his behavior as being inappropriate or perhaps fully proper, or somewhere in between.

The major difficulty with children evaluating their own conduct is that, in their desire to appear right, they refuse to "see" themselves honestly.

And it is here that the fully adult parent does not become vicious or insulting but reiterates the nature of the code violation ("You were wrong to take the change knowing it was incorrect.") and allows the child to rethink his conduct.

The younger the child, the less likely he is to accept his own obviously inappropriate behavior.

If you will remember that the good parent/therapist knows that growing up is a continuous process both for children and adults, then you will be able to make your point and let matters rest (unless the "resting" will result in grievous unhappiness to another).

In a very meaningful way parents indeed may consider themselves to be therapists.

Self-Image

A little child praying was heard to say: "Lord, I know I'm okay, cause God didn't make no junk."

Quite certainly, this child has an excellent self-image.

Self-image means nothing more than a child's picture of himself. As this picture develops so does his personality.

What a child believes about himself becomes more important than any of the "real" truths about himself.

For example, if he feels ugly, unlucky, unloved, unadmired, etc., that is truth for him, despite the fact that in the eyes of others none of what he felt and thought was true.

A child's self-image (like an adult's) is a complicated jig-saw puzzle. It is composed of many pieces.

One of these is his body image or his feelings about how he looks; another is his social image or his feelings about his social adequacy; others are his ability image, his intellectual image, his personality, character and finally his idealized image.

These component parts of the puzzle add up to his total self-image.

At many times in a lifetime there may be a temporary defective piece which too often is taken for the whole.

Thus, during adolescence a child's complexion may really be bad and his image of his body may, for awhile, be very bad.

If he considers all of his images negative because of the one defective piece, he is in emotional trouble.

The job of parenthood is to help the child manufacture a host of puzzle pieces which accumulate in a positive manner, finally adding up to a healthy self-image.

Growing up in a democratic, authoritative, affectionate, usually approving home atmosphere helps the child pile up positive self-images about his health, adequacy, sociability and intellectual functioning.

If he grows in this climate, he respects himself and holds few doubts about his general levels of functioning. Then he respects others, he is happy and is eventually free enough to be creative, autonomous and self-sufficient.

Here are ten ways to practically guarantee rearing a child who will hold a good image of himself.

1. Offer continual assistance, love and companionship without being asked for it.

2. Give ten or more minutes daily and individually to each child.

3. Express sympathy for a child's feelings.

4. Do things regularly *with* your child, not *for* him.

5. After disagreements, don't let silence simmer. Make up immediately stating your feelings clearly.

6. Remember all behavior is caused, so search for reasons with your child.

7. Don't unload physical or verbal abuse when you feel like exploding. Take a walk rather than teach your child any more immaturity than he already possesses.

8. Believe that your child wants to do the right thing even when he doesn't.

9. Praise everything you approve of liberally, and refrain as often as possible from paying too much attention to behavior you dislike.

10. Listen carefully often and long and try to hear what isn't being said.

That is all there is to it. You can rear a child with a strong self-image if you, the adult, really believe what you have just read, and if you are willing to practice what you believe to be correct.

Helping Children Become Competent

Helping children become competent is an important goal for parents.

Becoming competent very simply means acquiring skills— the skills of a personal nature (speech, listening, empathy, sympathy, etc.) and those of an impersonal nature (sports, hobbies, work, etc.)

Parents have to provide the opportunity for children to become competent. This does not necessarily mean expensive lessons. In fact, helping a child become competent can cost absolutely nothing or quite a bit, depending upon the parents' aspirations.

For example, a child's listening skills can be honed by playing simple games with him which demand that he listen, before his next move, to exactly what his opponent said.

Competency implies proficiency that the child recognizes. So, when he says, "I can shoot five baskets in a row," he is demonstrating that he knows he is competent in that particular area.

Competency breeds confidence, capacity and that all-important positive concept of self.

Confidence may breed contempt, even arrogance, but this is not necessarily so. Competency tempered with modesty and the desire to learn still more is the goal.

An important point to remember: When a child feels competent by child-like standards, adults should not compare his competency with other children's or with adults.

With his present feeling of success he will likely go on to achieve real competency. If his present level is degraded by comparison, he will likely never progress.

Helping children become competent is an exciting, rewarding and persistent parental task.

Don't Rush the Child

Americans are preoccupied with revving up the intellectual development of their children. There is no country in the world that is so saturated with this useless, inane ideology.

There is not a shred of evidence that says we can make any substantial difference in a child's intellectual future by the things we do early in his life.

Indeed, there is very little we can do to accelerate intellectual growth and output by any school practices. How patently naive can we be to think that through the use of "kits," and other mechanical devices, we can make any material difference in developing the intellect.

Jean Piaget, the Swiss psychologist whose formulations about the structure and development of children's intellectual powers has advanced our knowledge immeasurably, never envisioned anyone taking his formulations about development at each age level and capitalizing upon them by constructing materials which utilized the ideas.

Indeed, he has been profoundly shocked by what some American entrepreneurs have done with his theoretical formulations.

Of course, school and family life do affect intellectual growth. But there is little point in trying to accelerate intellectual development by courses, gadgets and doodads which attempt to capitalize upon the intellectual growth processes which Piaget has so carefully defined.

At a recent conference in New York here is exactly what Piaget did say: "If the aim (of intellectual kits based upon his theoretical conceptualizations) is to accelerate the development of children's thinking operations, it is idiotic." Later on he said, "I have a horror of teaching methods that are predetermined."

Designing paraphernalia around any person's theoretical ideas is dangerous because the theory is often confounded by the infinite variability of children.

Piaget has said that at certain ages in a child's life he appears to have the intellectual capacity to do only certain kinds of intellectual operations. For example, the average child is nearly 11 before he can deal with really abstract concepts. And you cannot train say a six-year-old to think as if he were 11.

There is still a valid orderliness (albeit there are variations in children) to the development of a child's thinking processes.

You can't make a frog out of a tadpole by cutting off its tail. You can't make an 11-year-old thinker out of any six or eight-year-olds by simply providing practice with a kit or other set of materials.

The effort isn't worth it either for parent or child.

"Let him live and be well," my mother would say, and you know she's right.

Appropriate Sex Roles

Sexual faddism has reached its height when the forces opposing the rigid definition of sex roles have all but obliterated the sex differences between children. I am regularly pummeled with literature which cries aloud that here is a new set of books with no sex differences whatever indicated.

Of course there are differences between boys and girls. And we have been too rigid. But if we ever tread the path towards negating any semblance of sex differences between children, we shall be doing irreparable harm to our youth. It is silly, extreme and unwise to completely neutralize children.

There are clear sex differences that have nothing whatever to do with cultural conditioning. One of these is anatomical. Try as we may there are and always will be physical differences between boys and girls. These differences often dictate style differences in dress, even expectations of performance.

Another sex difference is in the mortality rate, birth weight, proneness to disease, etc., between boys and girls with the edge always in favor of the girls. That is, girls die less frequently in the first year of life, they weigh more at birth, and they are less susceptible to disease than boys. There are other differences that are obvious to the trained eye.

This is not intended to mean that we should rigidly stereotype, separate and discriminate because of sex. Indeed, I am in favor of all equalization of opportunity, whether it be Little League or class-monitors.

Those mod young couples who are carried away with the idea that we have too long promulgated a sexist society, and vow to eliminate any sexual distinctions from their child-rearing, may rear children who really do not understand what or who they are.

Two sexes are basic to living. All of life depends upon the full realization that this is so. Eda Le Shan has put it this way: "When we interfere with boys being boys and girls being girls, we stunt the life force of the child."

A great part of normal human development depends upon the absolute and clear knowledge of one's sexual identity. Minimizing sex differences seems to have its place, but squelching sex differences is absurd adult behavior.

If perchance we convinced boys that they were girls, we would still have to face the fact that boys, for example, develop learning-to-read problems far more than girls. If we called a child "it" instead of "he" or "she," we could know the boys from the girls because of the differences in early learning ability.

It is a fact, then, that many sex differences are innate, deep down and very important developmentally. Should a child really be confused about his gender the severest kind of emotional difficulties will appear.

Mod parents are advised to establish sexual identity for their children. It would be ill-advised to prohibit all kinds of sex-related behavior. It would be equally foolhardy to act as if there were absolutely no differences between boys and girls.

I'm not sure there are activities that are only suitable for little girls—and that little boys should be prohibited from ever engaging in such behavior.

The most common fear of parents is that their little children will, if they are boys, want to dress up as girls. In and of itself this is not harmful at all, provided that parents do not perpetuate the myth because of their convictions about a sexist society.

Few little boys persist in this behavior unless there has been severe family "illness" such that his identification is with females.

Left to his own and without the approval of his parents he will soon revert to male dress. Homosexual behavior ordinarily does not mean that boys wish to be dressed as girls. A rejection of one's sex is, as far as I am concerned, a sign of emotional disturbance.

To be more definite: Parents should allow all kinds of behavior that appears to be more suitable to the opposite sex provided they do not make this an obsession.

That is, when parents too deliberately make their boys wash and cook and sew and skip rope just because they do not want to foist male sexism upon them, then they have foisted another kind of behavior.

If a little boy wants to play "mommy" or a little girl wants to be a "daddy," a hands-off approach would be advisable. What is natural in this case is good. We should no more think of telling a little boy not to cry because "only little girls do" than we should encourage a girl to cry because it is "lady-like."

In all cases of children under six not behaving as one would traditionally expect a person of that sex to behave, a cool and mildly observant attitude is suggested. Past the age of six, a cool and mildly observant attitude is also suggested.

Again, in the normally healthy family there is little reason to panic when little girls or boys don't act exactly as little boys and girls have always acted. In time, other things being equal, boys act like boys and girls like girls.

That's the way I see it. I do not see aberrant sexual behavior as simply an alternative lifestyle. By the same token I do not believe in witch hunts.

The Handicapped Child

There is almost nothing so heartbreaking to parents as to know that one of their children is in some way obviously different from other children.

In the case of a child with an easily identifiable deformity—a disease such as epilepsy, for example, or a speech or hearing handicap—there is at least one very important thing parents can do to help that child survive the ostracism and humiliation he will almost certainly face as he matures.

The child must get special help in learning. He must be taught particular skills, so that he can excel in some endeavor. This is absolutely necessary so that he can build enough self-esteem to withstand the rugged rejections that are on the horizon.

Unfortunately, children with an unattractive appearance, quirks of temperament or with intellectual or social limitations are almost certain to have a battle to hold their own outside of the family circle.

Generally, parents, in their desire to do the right thing, attempt to insulate the child from the hurts that will ensue.

In my own family there is a classic example. My niece is neurologically and physically handicapped in many ways.

My sister's first reaction was of pity and protection. My physician brother-in-law, made of sterner stuff, than the Landaus, knew that in order to assure the emotional survival of his daughter, she would have to learn and relearn things that most children learn and never forget.

And so he taught her, drilled her in fundamentals—and today, much to the amazement of us all, she is ready for driver training in a California high school.

As dispassionately as possible, parents need to assess the true status of a handicapped child (professional help may be useful at this point) and then select reasonable skills for the child to pursue.

Parents must then aggressively devise strategies for teaching these skills, in which, hopefully, the child can excel.

Naturally, it is a decided advantage if the child has an interest in a skill.

But if this is not so, then it is up to the parents to beg, cajole, bribe or force the child to start the learning process.

I use the word "force" because only adults can understand what may lie ahead—a child cannot be relied upon to be prescient about his future.

By the time a handicapped child is eight years old, his parents should have fairly well decided which skill or skills they will help him acquire. It may take sheer willpower on their part to insist, even force, him to learn that skill.

In the beginning stages of that learning, even tangible rewards may be condoned so that the child can surmount the obstacles of assimilating something new.

If in a year or less, the new skill doesn't catch on, then another must be substituted as vigorously as the last.

For the handicapped child, excellence in some area is absolutely necessary to build enough self-esteem so that he can withstand the rejection, or derision, of his peers.

The Morality Gap

In Birmingham, England, not too long ago, Sir Keith Joseph, home secretary in the British Conservative Party's shadow cabinet, said, "The worship of instinct, of spontaneity, the rejection of self-discipline, is not progress; it is degeneration."

In other words, the civilized values in the world, usually developed in families, are not outmoded. It is simply that they have been abandoned as explicit teachings in families.

Rather than attribute this remark to the expostulations of a man dreaming of a dimly recollected past, let me remind you that the Harvard psychologist, Dr. Jerome Kagan, once said that perhaps schools should give grades for altruism rather than reading.

Important as reading is, human decency in the form of altruism (the practice of unselfish concern or devotion to the welfare of others) is at least as important.

Nor is Kagan or Sir Joseph alone. In 1973 the psychiatrist, Dr. Karl Menninger, wrote a volume which sounds odd given the amoral context of today's American society. It was called, "Whatever Became of Sin?" (New York: Hawthorn Books).

When in 1971 Toynbee coined the term the "morality gap," in *Surviving the Future,* Oxford U. Press, he was referring to "man's giftedness for science and technology on the one hand and for religion and sociality on the other...."

Menninger, trying to explain the morality gap, says, "The popular leaning is away from notions of guilt and morality. Some politicians, groping for a word, have chanced on the silly misnomer, permissiveness.

"Their thinking is muddy but their meaning is clear. Disease and treatment have been the watchwords of the day and little is said about selfishness or guilt or the 'morality gap.' And certainly no one talks about sin!"

All this leads up to my plea for the family to take an active role in explicitly teaching children that there is right and wrong, that there are sins—against man, neighbors, environment, nations, family and friends.

Parents need not merely be examples. We have to sort out a certain degree of parental didacticism, and also their national dogmatism about what is and is not ethical.

Too many parents do not tell their children what is evil and good. They hope, pray and expect that morality will, like the measles, be caught. From where?

I do not know the complete answer. It is surely not from TV. It will surely not be caught from the movies. It cannot be ascertained from the newspaper accounts of Watergate.

The only place that can explicitly teach what is sinful in human relations is the home, where it is the solemn obligation of the parents to take upon themselves this task.

Let's face it. The explicit moral exhortations of the Rolling Stones and the folk singers are not frowned upon. Indeed, millions of children have found their moral leadership in rock groups.

And why shouldn't they? They get it nowhere else. Neither their schools, nor their homes, nor most of their churches offer overt moral guidance.

The "morality gap" is a parental problem. The intellectual world cannot, will not, and does not offer any answers. You, dear parents, do.

Importance of a Child's Moral Character

The anxiety of parents for the character development of their children is understandable.

There is no more important facet of human development than the cultivation of character.

No educational attainments, no economic success, no physical attributes can compare to the generally subscribed to consensus that "Jane has character."

Eons ago I stopped a young cousin of mine who had a sister my age and inquired about her sister's whereabouts that evening. She replied that Elaine was out with a young man named Herbert.

Herbert was known throughout our neighborhood as a young man with a very severe case of acne.

Before I could really register any sort of judgment about Elaine's companion this 11-year-old saucily said, "Well, Herbert may have pimples, but he has character."

By the age of six or seven it is possible for parents to make some determination regarding the character development of a child.

If a child is showing increasing signs of inner control, a strong sense of right or wrong, and an ability to identify with others, a parent may assume that normal character progress is being achieved.

If a child is developing inner control, he is able to withhold temper, to deny himself what he wants at the moment he wants it, and to show that he doesn't say everything he feels or means.

When a child knows the difference between right and wrong, he is able to label acts and judgments as being such. He should be able to verbally express and decide whether his response or someone else's is right or wrong.

As he watches TV he should show evidence that he recognizes correct and incorrect responses as they occur on the screen.

When a six-year-old shows that he relates to friends of his own age, to adults of various kinds—teachers, cousins, neighbors, sanitation men and even strangers—then he is demonstrating behavior which shows that he is able to relate to others in a meaningful way.

The opposite of any of these qualities is a sign of trouble. If a child shows estrangement from others, the inability to accept good and bad standards, a callousness towards animals and humans or an inability to play house, to play mother or father or just to play, parents ought to be aware enough to consult a professional who may be of help.

The Question of Obedience— Developing Character

Everybody wants obedient children. There can be no good society without some sources of authority. We expect our children, more or less, whether we be liberals, conservatives or middle-of-the-roaders, to obey authority to a reasonable degree.

Some years ago, a very perceptive and brilliant psychologist asked an extremely difficult question and performed a much-celebrated experiment about obedience.

Dr. Stanley Milgram of Yale University sat dozens of people down before a machine which was designed to administer an electric shock to a person who was unable to memorize certain pairs of words.

The machine was marked from 15 volts (mild shock) to 450 volts (dangerous shock), and triggered by 30 switches in a horizontal row.

The instructions to the person using the machine, given by an authoritative, white-coated scientist, were to "zap" the learner if he did not memorize certain pairs of words on a prescribed schedule. Every time a person made a mistake, he was ordered to increase the voltage and to "zap" the learner.

As the learner continued to make mistakes, he was "zapped" with increasingly larger shocks of electricity until finally he started to groan. A little later on he started to scream and said that he had recently had a heart attack and he couldn't stand it.

The question that Stanley Milgram wanted to answer was, "At what point would ordinary people stop giving increased dosages of electricity to people who were trying to learn paired words?" In other words, Milgram wanted to find out what happens when the demand of authority conflicts with conscience.

I have shown numerous classes the moving picture of Stanley Milgram's experiment.

Most frequently the person who was doing the zapping was indignant about having to do it because of the obvious distress of the learner (who was on the other side of the room in a glass-enclosed room). At this point, the stern scientist would step out and say, "You must continue, it's part of the experiment."

Did this stop anyone? The results were amazing and revolting. Milgram discovered that most people administering the test agonized, suffered, rationalized, yet obeyed the authority figure right down to the very last 450 volts severe shock treatment.

Almost two thirds of Milgram's subjects administered the highest levels of shock, even when they thought that the victim might be injured.

There is no denying the importance of authority in life. For the child to be subject to no authority figures is dangerous to the growth and development of his conscience and of his human relationships. The all-pervading issue that must be answered by each family is the degree to which they wish their children to be subject to authority which dictates being cruel to fellow human beings.

Milgram's work suggested that none of the people who administered the maximum severity of voltage could have been considered evil.

On the contrary, these were usually kind, considerate, moral and authority-conscious people. Their problem was not an innate cruelty or a learned cruelty, but the fact that when confronted by an anonymous authority figure, these ordinary human beings did the unthinkable.

The family is the place wherein the child learns obedience to authority. The family is also the place where the child must learn the limits to unrighteous authority.

When the child paintively cries, "But everybody else did it," then it is up to parents to carefully explain and to delineate the limits of authority. Children will not learn to refuse to obey the authority of evil people unless at home they are taught this.

The course of the world's history, both ancient and modern, might well have been changed by people who at one point in their lives as adults said, "No, this I shall not do. This is wrong."

Climbing and Character, 1

In my ceaseless search for those events in a child's life which are likely to build character, I journeyed recently to the Exum Climbing School in Moose, Wyoming.

I could not find a single instructor who had the conviction that rock climbing in and of itself would build character.

Despite my being singularly impressed with the utter devotion of the mountain climbing sport evidenced by the men I interviewed, I was surprised with their underestimation of their speciality.

Certainly, there are aspects of climbing which seem to be capable of nourishing the development of fine character.

However, like anything else of inherent value, one weekend of climbing discipline is not very likely to have any long, firm effect upon a child's character.

It was an expensive weekend to say the least. It cost $60 per person to climb the Grand Tetons and $35 per person for the two schools teaching, basic and intermediate climbing, which must be "passed" on separate days.

Having already "done myself in" four years ago, needless to say I bought the grub and tended the home fires in my waterless, bathroomless cabin in Wyoming. My son, Stewart, and cohort Charlie Winkle, climbed together.

As I view it, climbing (or any rugged outdoorsy sport) successfully demands intense interpersonal co-operation, personal determination, a concern for group safety, the testing of one's strength (mental and physical) and is a powerful means to validate the "conviction of being an individual who's center of gravity is within himself." (Adapted from the ideas in Hilde Bruch's "Learning Psycho-Therapy." Harvard University Press, 1974.)

My interview with a veteran instructor centered upon the qualities of character just described. When asked by the wife of one of the climbing instructors (to whom I described the purpose of my visit to the Tetons) what qualities of character every child should develop, I put it this way:

"Ideally every child should develop enough self-confidence that he is able to cope with his world without resorting to escape behavior. He should feel worthy and consider himself to be possessed of enough skills to enable him to guide his life with a reasonable rationality."

As I see it, the necessity of being indispensable to the safety of others, the grit needed to hang from rocks without knowing what lies below, and the feeling of immense accomplishment which comes from a grand ascent, all contribute to the development of the kind of character that turns children into more fully-functioning, self-actualizing adults."

Climbing and Character, 2

Climbing mountains is a valuable experience. As I see it, a climbing experience can have positive effects upon a child's sense of interpersonal co-operation, self-determination, his physical and mental strength.

It also reinforces his conviction that he is an individual with a center of gravity within himself.

My views on this subject were strengthened when I accompanied son Stewart and Charlie Winkle to Moose, Wyoming where they climbed the Grand Tetons in a party led by Don Mossman of the Exum Climbing School.

After, I spent a great deal of time trying to get a 16-year-old's (Charlie's) view of climbing.

Charlie feels there are four characteristics of personality which were indeed nourished by the experience he had climbing. These are admiration, compatibility, satisfaction and leadership.

His comments about each of these points follows:

Admiration—Charlie feels it is important for boys (and girls, of course...one of their party was a female in her early thirties) to locate adults whom they can admire. From admiration comes the desire to become. Until you want to become more than you are, there is no ambition.

Compatibility—I recall Glen Exum's speech to the party before they left for their two-day climb. He said, "If you don't suffer a bit, you haven't climbed the mountain."

Charlie feels that knowing your life depends upon the next man's rope skill lends to a real effort in the direction of compatibility rather than hostility.

Satisfaction—There is no doubt about it, everyone who climbed the Grand Tetons that day felt a surge of pride. Charlie says it sort of completed his boyhood. Another climber told me that nothing he had ever done was as satisfying.

Children need to feel deep strains of satisfaction about themselves as often as possible. Self-satisfaction breeds contentment.

Leadership—In mountain climbing skilled leadership is vital. The near-awe with which these boys looked at their guides was quite a thing to see. Yet, during any climb there is much opportunity for everyone to demonstrate leadership.

The key difference between this sport and the usual competitive sports where many of these same opportunities are available, is that in none of the others does leadership lead to life itself.

While there may be victory, there is not the satisfaction in knowing that your move on the rocks (in the game) made the difference between life and death.

Perhaps I am overenthusiastic about mountain stuff. I saw changes in two boys that I know they didn't see. Climbing the Grand Tetons brought two lads to the peak of themselves. It doesn't happen too often anywhere else.

Value of Competition

Much has been said in this nation about the spirit of competition. The strengths of the free enterprise system depend upon the competitive spirit.

However, deep within me I have the feeling that some of our shining hours have come, instead, from the cooperative spirit.

Because of my age I remember the significance of "Praise the Lord and Pass the Ammunition." I think of farmer's cooperatives, of people in floods[1] working together to rebuild homes and businesses.

Still there remains within me the realization that without some competitiveness in both the private and public sector there would be little cause at times to excel.

Children in school need some of the better things associated with pitting oneself against others.

---

1. The recent Teton Dam disaster (June, 1976) provides an excellent example of cooperative effort to achieve a common goal.

Even my friend, Herbie Kohl (the idol of the super-liberal educationists), said, "Some liberal teachers believe that all competitiveness should be removed from the classroom, that only cooperative games should be allowed. I don't feel that way. There is nothing wrong with occasionally testing yourself against someone else."

Competition is healthy when individual excellence needs stimulation. But pitting folks against other folks is bad when the only objective is victory at any cost.

Teachers and parents are able to arrange situations in which competitiveness does not maim or humiliate. It is even possible not to keep score. The aim of competition is to sharpen what we have—not to destroy the enemy.

I shall never forget the incident in Salt Lake City when a bakery burned. My friend, the owner of a competing bakery, allowed the owner of the burned-out establishment to use his facilities when his employees had finished their baking for the day.

Instead of gloating that another competitor had "bit the dust," there was a spirit of help within the framework of competition.

Good schools and families allow competition, but they must be certain that it doesn't erode the ego. Competition permeated with affection, where the winner does not take all, and where the loser is able to still hold his head high, can never hurt.

In every society the winners and the losers are known. In any classroom it doesn't take long to tell who the sharper children are. Even in the most vicious sport of all, boxing, we don't pit individuals against one another if their weights are vastly different.

Still, competition within reasonable "weight" limits is healthy.

It has been said that money is the root of all evil. Not true. It is the love of money which is pernicious.

Competition, per se, is not evil. It is the adoration of competition that is bad.

Toys—Blocks to Creativity

Not too many Christmases ago, while I was exploring the toy department of a local store, I found myself being trailed by a melee of mothers who were eagerly wanting to know what toys "made sense."

Remembering this incident has prompted me to write about toy-choosing, basing my recommendations upon some well-tested principles of child growth and development:

Rule number one: The fewer the toys, the better for the child's process of selectivity. He can be overstimulated by so many toys that none of them really gets used.

It is only adult willpower which may prevail in this matter. One of the more serious Christmas problems is parental fear of appearing to be tightwads if they don't rain toys upon their children's heads.

Discretion is truly the better part of valor in this matter.

Rule number 2: If it has batteries, forget it. I make this an absolute rule because toys should be energized by the humans who use them. Batteries guarantee that nothing creative can come from the toy. If you like a battery-powered toy, that's fine—but do not insert the batteries.

Rule number 3. Play is the purpose of toys. This requires the child to *do* something with the toy rather than merely watch it perform.

I object to autos that run around on any kind of tracks, unless it is possible for the child to add to the tracks and develop his own series of bypasses or obstacles. He may then play as if he were someone really using the track.

Rule number 4: All war-like toys—tanks, bombers, machine guns, radar sets, rifles, pistols and the like—are "no-no's" for me because they imply a value in combat. Only the most extreme elements of our gun-approving society would seriously feel that children should be taught that war is good.

Combat in self-defense seems to me to be obviously necessary, but war toys for children propagate an insensitivity to killing because the object of the toys is to "kill someone dead." I feel precisely the same way about GI Joe dolls. Barbies in war regalia aren't better dolls.

Rule number 5: The toy's other purpose, besides play, is to stimulate the child's imaginative powers so that he can add to the restricted dimension of the toy. A toy that does too many things for the child does not give him a chance to talk to the toy, to re-design it for his use. Building blocks serve this purpose excellently.

It is not unlike the difference between reading a book and seeing the movie about the book. In the latter case, all of your powers of imagination are stunted because the director has made the characters and places in his own image rather than allowing you the delightful experience of self-imagination.

Only in "Gone With the Wind" does anyone appear to be satisfied that Gable really was Rhett Butler.

Rule number 6: Usually the least expensive, most unattractive toys are the very ones which can make a significant difference in the play life of the child.

I hope you consider these rules most seriously. I have just cut your Christmas toy budget by 60-70 percent. Take that money and do something sweet for someone who hasn't been sweetened by anyone for a long time. Your children will benefit from the Christmas morning "scarcity," especially if they are under six.

If Christmas is a time of giving, then give toys to your child which will enlarge his creative powers, sharpen his ability to interact with the inanimate, and help him to understand himself better and the world in which he lives.

Helping Children Become Independent

Fostering independence in children is an important goal for parents.

Along with helping their children gain a useful self-understanding and become competent, parents should encourage them to become independent.

The following example shows how necessary this is:

A sixth grade child I observed a few years ago would not leave his mother's side on the first day of the new school year.

He was eleven, tall and handsome, but behaved in an exceptionally diffident manner.

Research shows that his mother had always been overprotective and never let him reach out gradually. Everything in his world came from and through his mother's hands.

In other words, she did not encourage independence in any way.

It takes some conscious parental behavior to insure that children at all ages have an appropriate degree of freedom so that they feel a gradual sense of independence. It isn't easy for parents to "let go" of their children.

Briefly reviewed, the parents of infants need not be overly concerned about independence; their primary aim is to give succor to their offspring. But from 18 months on, there is the persistent problem of gauging how much freedom and independence is consistent with the child's desires and his safety.

In general, we should allow as much independence as possible, always balancing the degree of latitude with the overall welfare of the child.

As the child moves into early adolescence and peer pressure to "do" things increases dramatically, his parents face a particularly difficult challenge.

If, indeed, the parent has been overly restrictive about granting independence commensurate with the child's age and maturity level, then two problems may occur.

First, the adolescent may not be able to comfortably join other peers who have been functioning quite independently; or second, the adolescent will suddenly demand more independence than he can handle and more than his parents are willing to allow.

An objective of normal human growth is the gradual separation from the generation that bore the child.

Autonomy and independence increase when parents realize what is meant by the terms and what they must consciously and consistently do to nourish their gradual development.

Self Reliance

Parents play a vital role in fostering a self-reliant attitude in a child.

Commencing with the age of three or four, a child can really do many more things for himself than we imagine.

On the other hand, a child wants and needs to know that if help is needed, parents will not stubbornly refuse it in the name of developing self-sufficiency.

Parents need to study each child enough to know whether crying and pleading are merely attention-seeking, or whether the child, in fact, cannot do something for himself.

There are a number of rejoinders for you parents wanting to develop greater self-reliance.

You can tactfully decline to help a child by saying such things as: "I'm not sure, what do you think?"..."Give it a try"... "I'll help you if you have trouble"..."You can do it"..."Have you thought of trying it this way?"

For a child to develop greater self-reliance, the adults in his life must continually encourage and approve his self-reliant behavior.

You stimulate such behavior if you, the parents, say: "Nicely done"..."You came close this time"...or "That was a good try."

One note of caution: If you withhold comments of a positive nature waiting for your child's definite, observable achievement, it is very likely there will be no achievement.

A practical point to remember: Your child will become self-reliant more easily if you help him along the way. For example: Put a stool in the bathroom or kitchen so the young child can easily get drinks and wash his hands.

Have an easy-to-reach shelf, where cups, napkins, and utensils are readily obtainable.

Place hooks in the closets so he can reach his clothes without help.

For the older child: Provide an alarm clock so that he can get up by himself.

Provide a house key so that he can let himself in if necessary.

And remember, in helping your child achieve self-reliance, make sure that the tasks he undertakes are not too difficult for his stage of development.

Help him to achieve success, so that he will want to continue being self-reliant.

A Son, Not a Friend

I suppose it had to happen. Everything in the books says it will—but when it does, it hurts. It's funny being a victim of theory. It isn't so funny when it happens to you.

My son is just past 15. For at least 10 years we have been companions in many places. We've climbed the Tetons together; we've skied hills I couldn't quite make; we've fought bitterly on the tennis court, and we've just done the many things that fathers and sons do when they "hang around" together. We're the only two men in the house.

It's like this...when I have to run an errand, record radio programs, pick up a new tire, or pop down to the store to get some extra milk, I usually take Stewart along. And he usually goes quite willingly. So, things are about what they have been in the past between us. It's been kind of nice for me, and I hope for him.

And then came the other day. Casually I turned to my son and said, "Hey, how about getting up early tomorrow morning and checking out the hills behind the University Hospital. It's a good walk. I need the exercise."

The bombshell—said he to me, "Look, I'm your son, not your friend. Find guys your own age to "hang out" with, OK?"

You know, that's exactly what is supposed to happen. As a child reaches his own maturity peaks he is supposed to separate from his folks and carve out his new life. Some have called it "autonomy." Others call it "independence."

Whatever it is, it's good for children to grow away from their parents so that they can enter into worlds of their own making. I know this well. I've taught it for years. But experiencing it hurt. It was a 'good' hurt, but for the moment it did hurt.

The purpose of being a father is to produce in one's son his ability to become a father (in the psychological sense). Letting go is an urgent step in the relationship between parents and all of their children. When children are able to easily leave their parents, it is a sign that the parents have done a good job.

I think I made somewhat of a mistake. My son and I had developed a symbiotic relationship over the years. That is, we were mutually dependent. In other words, my son depended upon me for many things...companionship, love, guidance and such. But I had unknowingly developed a dependence upon him for companionship, and he had become my sports partner and general buddy. When the inevitable and healthy break came, I wasn't prepared, but *he* was.

The only thing that saved me from being utterly embarrassed at my own stupidity was that I had helped to rear him so that he felt free to say what he did. Sons who cannot act in this way, as they move into full-blown adolescence, are overly dependent upon their fathers, or upon both parents, and thus their development has been stunted.

I have pulled myself together somewhat, and I am preparing to face my world more without Stewart than with. He is preparing for his own Odyssey. My role will be to be there when he needs me.

Every father must realize that his sons (and daughters) were not brought up to be there when he needs them.

"Your children are not your children.

"They are the sons and daughters of Life's longing for itself.

"They come through you but not from you,
"And though they are with you yet they belong not to you."

—K. Gibran

Parenting — Necessity of Maturity

Parents are made, not born. Too often, children become parents.

One of the major arguments against marriage in the teen years is that one has to be quite fully launched as an adult in order to be prepared to become a parent.

At least, one should evince clear indications that the process of maturation is being pushed along with normal speed.

Young people should look for reasonable maturity in a prospective marriage partner, rather than the outward signs of suitability, such as beauty, wealth and talent.

Birth control methods aside, when there is marriage, there is always the possibility and desirability of having children.

Despite certain avant-garde factions who insist that couples may deliberately opt not to become parents, the fullest flowering of marriage consists of the children born to that union.

The most important thing new parents can learn is that their own behavior as a couple is paramount in determining the personality development of their children.

Raising happy and stable children is less technology and more interparental relations than anyone might imagine.

More baldly put, the happier a marriage, the less chance there is for children to grow into trouble. The Biblical admonition that, like trees, children grow as they are bent means that the closest influence upon them, their parents, are also the greatest "bending forces."

Dr. Howard Lane used to say, "Good neighborhoods produce good children." It has taken me these many years to comprehend that he didn't always mean geographical neighborhoods. The most immediate neighborhood surrounding children is their immediate family.

Having children is worthwhile. It is the most completing experience any two individuals who marry will ever have. It transcends sexual appetite. It makes wealth and power seem small.

Parenthood is likely the underlying key to all human happiness. It is this concept that allows for great sacrifice and pain, so that a child may be born and develop well.

Who and what the parents are and how they relate to each other create fundamental forces upon their children.

Without maturity, children who become parents are often not much different than they were when they were playing with dolls.

6

The Influence of the Family

What Produces the Delinquent Child?

It is normal for parents to worry about their children, lest disrespect, disinterest and lack of obedience become deliberate and a sign of future delinquency.

Too often parents blame misbehavior on a child's self-centeredness and character rather than on immaturity. They often react violently towards misbehavior, which never really gets at the root of it.

Let's take a look at those conditions which lead to the child becoming the delinquent who runs afoul of the law. Remember that almost all of us have engaged in some delinquency in our youth, and sometimes in our adulthood. But to produce the child who appears before a court because of a long series of offenses there must have been antecedent conditions.

At least one or more (often, two or three) of these conditions must persist in order to eventually produce the delinquent youngster:

1. The child is subjected to heavy physical punishment, abuse and belittlement. Few children become delinquent because they were, on occasion, handled badly by their parents. Usually, there has to be a long and continuous history of lack of parental concern.

2. One or both parents are lacking in warmth, sympathy and affection. Juvenile authorities report that time and time again, youngsters who appear before them have parents who, in more than verbal ways, show that they couldn't care less about their children because after all, they are so "bad."

3. The child is consistently neglected and uncared for. It takes a heap of neglect to cause delinquency. All children can stand occasional parental neglect and what seems to be uncaring behavior.

When parents are consistently uncaring and consistently neglectful of the child's welfare, we may expect that this, in conjunction with the other conditions, will lead to delinquency.

4. The parents strongly prohibit aggression toward themselves, but often condone it toward others.

It is a curious thing to note that the parents of severely delinquent children seem to refuse to allow any kind of misbehavior, disrespect or otherwise neglectful behavior on the part of their children for them, but frequently approve of this kind of behavior and indeed, show it towards others in the family and community.

5. The parents themselves have numerous emotional problems and a lack of esteem for each other. It has often been said that the best present the child can receive from his parents is to see that his parents love one another.

Delinquency doesn't take place because of isolated loss of temper on the part of one or both parents.

The parents of delinquent youth usually are overladen with emotional problems of their own and couldn't care less about one another.

6. One or both parents are excessively hostile. Frequently, the parents of delinquent children are themselves, delinquents. They show persistently hostile attitudes towards all kinds of authority and thus feed the hostility of their children.

7. Fathers tend to ridicule boys when they make mistakes.

It has been my observation that in the attempt to make our children better, we fathers are too often hypercritical of everything our sons do. It is simply a common fact that no child can catch a ball as well as his father, conduct his daily affairs with the aplomb of his father, behave respectfully towards property as his father always does, and so on.

And thus, in an attempt to make a better son, fathers too often apply standards to their little boys that are unethical, unreasonable, and unjustifiably harsh. The sharpest kind of criticism is verbal ridicule from fathers who make fun of their children when they do not toe the mark precisely.

8. Few delinquents have close ties with their fathers. The evidence that has accumulated over the years indicates that one of the hallmarks of delinquent youngsters is that they show very few close affectional bonds with their fathers. In fact, a great deal of hostility is evident.

Let me emphasize that occasional physical punishment, occasional lack of affection, occasional emotional problems on the part of parents and occasional hostility towards the society around us will never produce the delinquent. The delinquent child comes from a persistent and consistent compounding of these conditions.

It is my belief that a child can tolerate nearly any kind of momentary aberration on the part of parents provided that the fault is surrounded by a wealth of concern, sympathy, affection and enhancement for that child's personality.

Don't kid yourself or anyone else. Your child will not become a delinquent because you make an occasional slip in good behavioral management. He will become a delinquent if you exemplify repeatedly at least two to three of the items we have just discussed.

Honest but loving parents can make a lot of mistakes rearing their children and still produce great youngsters. No one can shrug off the list of eight parental behaviors that are certain to result in delinquency.

The Influence of the Family on Drug Uses

In 1972 Richard Blum concluded his monumental study entitled, "Horatio Alger's Children" (San Francisco: Jossey-Bass Publishers).

His major conclusion was that it is possible to identify the characteristics of excellent, good and bad families, and that one could predict the risk a child might incur in the direction of drug abuse and use based upon the type of family from which he came.

In fact, Blum not only says that one can predict drug risk based on family factors but maintains that other factors hardly enter.

In other words, despite the recent cry that peers influence children unduly (Urie Bronfenbrenner, "Two Worlds of Childhood: U.S. and U.S.S.R." New York: Russell Sage, 1970), Blum stoutly maintains that an intensive look at family dynamics shows clearly that children from good families and children from excellent families do not get as seriously involved in drug use or abuse as children from families rated as troubled or pathological.

Earlier I alluded to what has been termed peer group domination in the literature on drug users. That is, it was as if nothing parents said or did mattered. If a child's friends used, so did he.

Blum's intense examination of families of children who were high and low risk drug users definitely contradicts the entire notion of the peer group having the final say.

Though Blum does not argue about the enormous influence of peers in school performance or agression and cheating, he does explicitly say that his data regarding drug risk is almost entirely related to the family's rating.

To quote Blum exactly makes the point even more emphatic: "All children in our study demonstrated how important their parents' love is to them. Some stated this explicitly; some showed it through resentment and misbehavior when they felt abandoned by their parents; some merely implied it through the high price they were paying to maintain their parents' regard. Clearly, the parents were the dominant force in their lives—whether the child was seriously disturbed or ebulliently well-adjusted."

What Blum has said squares precisely with my own experience with drug addicts in many parts of the country. High drug-risk children come from sick family interaction patterns.

It has been my experience that too many parents feel that their kids do not hear them. Oh, they listen, but do not hear.

Blum avers that children hear very well. As Blum says, "The problem, then, is in the message, since it is sure to be received."

Family, Fun and Drug Use

In "Horatio Alger's Children," Blum drew certain conclusions about the families of children who were classified as high-risk (most likely to use) drug offenders.

I was particularly impressed that in all three types of families classified by Blum (superior, average and troubled) the children demonstrated through actions and words that their parents' love for them was very important.

Further, Blum found that parents' messages do get through to their children.

In many ways all three types of families were very much alike on many criteria. Blum says, "The major difference between the three groups was the degree to which they had fun together—not in the strength of the bond.

"Happiness and pleasure within the family circle were characteristic of superior and good families." On the other hand, troubled families were characterized by pain and humiliation.

Superior families were evidenced by a lack of aggression, friendly firmness of the parents, and self-assurance. Superior families rewarded their children for having strong yet differing opinions from their parents and there was a great deal of frankness among them.

It is instructive to read what various parents in families rated superior (very low drug-risk for their children) said about their family relationships:

"We have a lot of love...respect. If a child is getting love and understanding at home, he does not have to get acceptance in his peer group. We have very hot discussions. The generation gap is there. But when we go to bed, even though we hadn't solved it, we had our ideas and they had theirs...we kissed; we agreed to disagree and still respect each other for that. One of the ways you can show love is to be actually a father and a mother to your children...we are their parents. Love is not being permissive and kind at all times. The strongest love you can have for your children is the love where you take the time to be tough; and once in a while even use your foot to give them a good swift kick, but everything is tempered by love."

I don't know if one book can convert a family into a happy, humorous crew. I do know that the strongest evidence of a superior family is the fun they have together in spite of differences, in spite of parental battles which are always patched, in spite of sometimes vigorous discipline.

All any reader needs to do is double check his family, not for cohesion, not for sharing identical views, not for outward appearances, but for a basic love of fun and life that exists despite stormy battles.

Inner joy and strength are what make low-risk children. When children feel these elements, almost any kind of family surface things may occur with little harm to them.

Children who feel the deep contentment of their parents, in spite of outward disagreements, even battles, need not search for meaning in life outside of their family culture.

It is only when basic harmony and discontent prevail that children search for elusive meanings and gratifications. The drug culture offers them plenty of that type of meaning.

The absence of love, charity, humor, respect, tolerance, confidence and joy in a family nearly dooms an adolescent to seek his happiness and comraderie in the lovelessness of drugs.

Predicting Drug Use

In 1970 Dr. Urie Bronfenbrenner said in a "Time" interview: "The battle today is not between children and parents; the battle is between society on one side and families on the other."

The subtitle of Blum's "Horatio Alger's Children" referred to earlier was "The Role of the Family in the Origin and Prevention of Drug Risk." Its conclusions are not the least bit surprising. In effect, the drug use of certain children can be predicted with startling accuracy by studying their families.

Blum was able to divide families into two major categories— high risk (it was demonstrated that their children were more likely to be drug-users) and low risk. There were two kinds of families identified—the traditional and authoritative and the permissive.

Traditional and authoritative families were defined as those where the father has an authoritative role, where the family emphasizes obedience and self-control in their children, and where they create tightly integrated, interdependent family units.

Permissive families emphasize the child's flexibility and freedom, believing that the child needs to grow and develop to do "his own thing" in this world.

Research results showed that in traditional (authoritative) families there is a low risk of unhappy drug outcomes. In permissive families there is a high risk of illicit drug use.

Uncorrelated to this finding is the interesting fact that high risk families appear to use more prescribed medication and have more alcohol and tobacco on hand than low risk families.

High risk families have children that are more knowledgeable about drugs, while low risk children appear insulated from the influence of drug-using peers, even though they live in neighborhoods and go to schools where illicit drugs are readily available.

It would appear then, that we have as a generation, "copped out" of familial responsibility and placed all the blame for all of the things that happen to our children on the heads and shoulders of their peer group.

When parents know what they believe, and enunciate these beliefs with love, patience, moderation and understanding, then the children develop an attachment to these family values and at least are able to pit them against that peer group.

Among the white, middle-class families the high risk were less religiously involved, put less emphasis on child rearing, belief in God, and self-control than did low risk families.

High risk families also gave greater freedom to children, formed less cohesive family groups, showed more evidence of alcohol use and demonstrated more permissive attitudes towards the activities of their children.

What can we justifiably conclude. Some of you will not like to hear this. The "square" family where there is not absolutism is the best safeguard against drug abuse by children.

The more libertine the parental attitude the greater the risk of drug use for the child brought up with few fences.

To Consult, Console and Cajole, 1

There wasn't anyone (or at least it seemed) in the Bronx River Parkway that afternoon who didn't look enviously at the sleek Silver Shadow Rolls Royce as it made its way majestically towards Scarsdale, New York.

As I sat in the rear of the vehicle listening to the pitiful story of those who owned it, I could only recall that I'd heard the story many times before.

It was Sunday, December 15, 1974. I had just completed another meeting of the board of directors of Odyssey House in New York City. And some of us had just finished talking about how rich parents too often unknowingly live in worlds which exclude their children.

And that is precisely what happened to the Richmonds.

Moments before, we were sitting with their son, Richard, now a resident of Odyssey House, a full-time psychiatrically oriented drug-free therapeutic community. (There is one in Salt Lake City, Utah.)

Mrs. Richmond is sleek, richly clad in flowing mink and now, a new woman. Mr. Richmond is imperially slim, elegantly manicured, and he, too, is a man reborn. Mrs. Richmond now works full time for Odyssey as an unpaid volunteer. Mr. Richmond serves on the board of directors with me.

These parents, occupying the svelt world of the very rich, were, until a year ago, so self-absorbed in their cocktail-party-circuit lives that they never really "saw" or "felt" their two children.

And Dick, their only son, found himself in search of himself with neither parent to consult, console or cajole.

Somehow, they report, they were all strangers to one another. At least until that terrible moment that the light knock on the door told them that their son was at the station house arrested for selling drugs.

A recent article in the New York Post (Tuesday, December 17, 1974) by Edmund Newton, concerned itself with the whys and wherefores of male teen-age hustlers on 4nd Street.

Quoted in this article is 16-year-old Malo Cruz (not rich, not from "too busy" parents) who, when asked about his male prostitution said what I think sums up the intent of this article: "It's not necessarily a matter of kids leaving their homes, some homes leave their kids."

All of this may leave you with two not entirely erroneous conclusions. One is that parents who are "out" too much cause their children to seek company elsewhere; the other is that it is only the cocktail-drinking folks who produce addicted children.

Neither statement is untrue. Yet, neither is the whole truth.

You may be "out" much, and still when you're "in," you may be able to lovingly consult, warmly console and sharply cajole—and thus prevent your children seeking solace from peers who have been "left" by their homes.

In this case, drugs offer the golden opportunity to blot out a belligerent, cold and hostile world. Indeed it is true that most drug addicts report one or both parents as inveterate drug-takers—either alcoholics or tranquilizer addicts.

My own experience with drug addicts forces me to conclude that rich or poor, when children see their parents as self-absorbed, hedonistic maniacs who daily roam the better boutiques in an incessant search for the "chic," "in" things to wear and buy whatever they fancy, or who while away their time and money in alcoholic stupors oblivious to their children's lives, these children respond by zonking out on this scene.

Equally serious are parents who shift the parental responsibility onto public and church institutions.

In short, whatever parents do that separate them emotionally from their children makes fertile ground for the seeds of addiction.

To Consult, Console and Cajole, 2

Each word is very important to the eventual well-being of every child. In combination they are a certain formula for preventing the onset of a disease known as drug addiction.

"Consulting" is that effort made by parents to regularly (daily) inquire about the lives of their children.

This consciously-motivated activity, when done in the spirit of love and concern and not as an attempt to accuse, tells children that their parents are continually interested in their lives.

I consider it of paramount importance that, as families grow larger, the frequency, intensity and magnitude of the concern be even greater than before.

Most of what I see is after-concern. That is, after there's trouble, parents begin to wake up and become consulting. When parents view their role as full-time consultants to their children they will have amply demonstrated their concern.

What to do?

1. Deliberately, consciously and in a one-to-one relationship, seek out each child daily for a "free" consultation.

2. Do it away from the madding crowd.

3. Don't do anything else while you are a consultant.

4. Check with your spouse to be certain you are, in fact, being a consultant and not a Gestapo agent.

After consulting comes consoling.

Every child needs someone to enfold him in concern as he "treads the primrose path of dalliance."

All children (except very emotionally ill ones) need, from birth onward, to know that their parents may not approve (see the discussion below on "cajoling") of what they do but that they will commiserate and empathize with the child.

What to do?

1. Whenever kids are in trouble, get close to them and down to them, enfold them and listen.

2. Mirror their feelings, even if you don't share them (e.g., "I'll bet you were disappointed" or "That must have hurt.")

3. While not excusing, you need to verbally reassure them that they aren't irrevocably "lost."

4. Love and hold them long enough so that they say "It's enough: I'm O.K."

When we cajole, we explicitly tell children what we approve and disapprove of. There is no parental shame to be suffered when children know their parents' code of behavior.

Super-liberal (not in the political sense) parents feel that a code of behavior is something that should not be foisted upon the child. If you don't "foist" first, someone else will.

There is no shame in expressing distaste or disapproval for children's acts you disapprove of. Children do not grow values alone. If you blithely wait until they are "of age" so they can choose their path, they will already have chosen someone else's value system, and you'll be out in left field.

What do do?

1. Along with consulting and consoling you need to express approval and disapproval of children's behavior.

2. Be proud if a child says, "I didn't do it because I knew you'd be hurt."

3. Enunciate more positive views of human conduct, so that children can feel the pattern of value structure in a positive light.

4. Decide, as a couple, which values in life you will exemplify and approve of.

Afterwards, take every opportunity to consciously and consistently inculcate those values (e.g., "That man was really decent. See how he stopped to let that car into line," or "You just were very honest in your dealings with your sister. I am proud of you.")

Youth and Drug Abuse

In 1970 Walter Vandermeer died of an overdose of heroin 15 days after his 12th birthday.

Antoinette Dishman, a bright 17-year-old black girl, was dead from a heroin overdose taken at a party.

Ralph deJesus, age 12, entered a drug program.

In testimony before the New York Joint Legislative Committee on Protection of Children and Youth and Drug Abuse, he so moved the audience with his poignant story that some legislators had to leave the room before they broke down in front of their peers.

It is now 1978. Even though folks would like to believe that America's drug problem has silently slipped away, it just isn't true.

With Turkish governmental restrictions lifted on the growing of heroin, even in Salt Lake City we are feeling the effects. Just the other night it was reported that one of the "big" local pushers had been arrested. Sad to say the end of heroin is not nearly in sight.

There was a time when we equated heroin use with Vietnam. There was despair over the ugly war. Children caught their elders' disgust and dropped out of life by using heroin. At least, that is what we thought.

We have known for a long time that heroin use is not necessarily related to poverty, international crisis and government turmoil. In my opinion, attributing heroin use to world conditions is a genuine copout. It is clear and simple. I have said it before but it always bears repeating:

When children discover that their folks don't care, when they find out that almost everything and anything is okay with their modish parents, and when they realize the awful discrepancies between parental words and deeds, they are so hurt, so humiliated, so unable to cope that they enter the dream world of hard drugs.

After years of dealing intimately with drug addicts of all ages I make the following statements without any reservations or fear of being contradicted:

A child on drugs is not a problem as much as he is a *symptom* that something is not right at home. This has nothing whatever to do with religion, social class or educational level.

Of course, it is true that the child's peers or friends pressure him to just try it once.

Of course, it is true that there are periods of deep disillusionment in adolescents. But an adolescent's armor is forged at home long before adolescence rolls around.

Community drug programs, adult concern and school attempts to slow the pace of addiction are doomed to failure because they look at drug addiction as a problem.

If driver education is important, and it is, how much more important is parent education?

Driver education treats driving as a thing one must do *before* things get out of hand on the road.

Similarly, all children in the public schools must be exposed to some of the basic ingredients of child-rearing and family life. Where is it written that automobiles are more important than people?

It is not too late. Drug addiction is not something in our memories of yesteryear.

The threat of drug addiction is not relegated to bad neighborhoods. It is not someone else's problem.

It is your problem *now* in your home, especially if your children are under 12.

High Risk Children

Human beings, it seems, are always in quest of the impossible. When Robert Peterson sings "The Impossible Dream" or when Ponce de Leon searches vainly for the fountain of youth, they are, in reality, all of us in our search of perennial happiness or perfect mates.

Most parents wish they had some accurate gauge with which to predict the success or failure of their children.

There are eight categories of temperament which, if carefully studied, can help (but *not* predict with a certainty) a parent determine whether or not their preschool-age child should be given some professional attention.

Activity Level—Children with high activity level are often seen as very annoying to adults. When they are dashers and prancers in the home, they knock things over and cause turmoil. Parents often continually equate their activity with being "bad." If this is overdone, the child learns to be disobedient.

On a scale of high, moderate and low you are in no trouble with a medium level and could be in some difficulty with an extreme of either of the other two.

Rhythmicity—The regularity and predictability of feeding patterns, elimination and sleeping are called the child's rhythm. A certain regularity in each of these areas is important.

Approach or Withdrawal—When a child reacts to new stimuli with consistent withdrawal, rather than moving toward new things, it may be something to watch more carefully. Quite obviously when the previous two temperaments, in either extreme, combine with withdrawal, parents need to be on the alert.

Persistent withdrawal is not obstinacy but a characteristic of temperament which is deviant.

Adaptability—Emotional and physical accommodation to new circumstances or stressful situations may be accomplished slowly or rapidly.

There may be an initial period of time when there is little adaptability, such as at the opening of school.

Should a child continually show an inability to adapt to new environments, and if this is coupled with any or many of the already discussed temperaments, then a parent should be on the lookout for the development of a behavior disorder.

Quality or Mood—If the way a child reacts to most of life's events is particularly negative rather than pleasant, joyful and friendly, then his mood is essentially dissonant.

The most troublesome factor about this is the response his temperament evokes from those around him. Ordinarily, few adults will tolerate the withdrawing, maladaptable, sullen child.

When he gets this message of non-acceptance, he exhibits anti-social behavior.

Intensity of Reaction—In general children are mild, average or intense in their reactions to life's "goodies." So, when disappointment is faced, not with a whimper but with a resounding temper tantrum, a child has an especially tense, negative response to conditions. When joy is expressed with shrieks of delirium, a child has an overly-exuberant response.

In each case the responses of the adult world will help predict what may eventually happen to the child's accommodation to his fellowmen.

Threshhold of Responsiveness—Unusual sensitivity to stimuli, such as not responding for a long period of time to auditory or visual cues, is often a source of wonder, fear and annoyance in adults. When children are overresponsive, this too produces adult fears.

Distractibility—Children who rarely complete tasks are often particularly distractible. They are easily diverted from a certain path. In general, parents cannot abide it, although it is quite normal. Again, extreme distractibility usually evokes intense adult response.

Attention Span and Persistence—This category is closely related to the one just above. Adults usually approve of those children with longer attention spans because they stick to tasks.

If a child exhibits all or most of the above negative temperaments, it might be wise to seek help. Remember, all children show all of these temperaments at one time or another. Family responses are what make the difference in producing the child with a behavior disorder.

Even a child with a few extreme responses may grow up reasonably well if the adults and peers in his life accept him. The child has a high risk of developing a behavior disorder if these temperaments are extreme and rejected.

Parents Set the Example

In a neighboring state there was a sticker placed upon a cigarette vending machine that said: "Minors are prohibited by state law from purchasing cigarettes from this machine. PARENTS WILL PLEASE COOPERATE."

I remembered this when recently I was made aware of a number of juveniles who, taking advantage of the absence of parents of one of the "gang," used their home to party. In the process they stole a car belonging to the couple and did damage to the interior of the house.

Upon arriving home the parents were appalled at the damage done to their property. In vain they waited for any of the parents of the offending juveniles to come forth with some explanation or offer some help.

It was as if nothing had ever happened, yet the parents of every child involved were contacted and made aware of the havoc.

It is evident that these parents, rather than passing on to their children a code of conduct were, in fact, inspiring disorderliness.

This is not the place to validate the claims and counterclaims related to the incident.

However, assuming that the events I have described did take place in one form or another, it is enough to establish a correct principle. That principle is that parents must, even if it hurts, stand squarely on the principle that there is a right and a wrong in their children's behavior with regard to person and property.

It is the solemn duty of parents to confront children with their wrongdoings and exact penance and penalty. Not to protest the wrongdoings of children negates the essence of proper child-rearing.

You may recall the column I wrote about children who were guilty of cheating a gas station operator by accepting change from $10 when they knew they had given only $5. The children favored the expression, "Caveat vendor" ("Let the seller beware").

An alert parent immediately dispatched the "pirates" to the scene to return the stolen funds.

Parents with true values do not accept catch phrases which seek to excuse wrongdoing with pretenses.

The sins of commission are particularly heinous. By doing and saying nothing parents actually become accessories to larceny. The harvest they will reap is not a miscreant son but generations of humans who will inspire their children to neglect the basics of human decency.

The Indignities of Childhood

When the biographies of 12 Nazi leaders were written in a volume entitled, "The Face of the Third Reich" (Pantheon Press,) 1970) a startling discovery emerged. Nearly all of these convicted criminals had suffered some sort of serious mistreatment or cruelty in childhood.

Leopold Bellak, M.D., has written that "Man's inhumanity to man is his revenge for the indignities he suffered in childhood."

It is curious that despite the general disrepute of Freudian theory that pervades the psychological profession today, volume after volume, research piece after research piece seem to reiterate a common Freudian theme: that which we experience in childhood leaves an indelible mark upon our lives.

At least one of the murderers in the Texas sex-crime spree of Wayne Henley and his cohorts came from a family where the father regularly came home from drunken orgies to beat his wife and all of the children.

Walter Langer's classic study of the life of Adolf Hitler, "The Mind of Adolph Hitler" (New York: Basic Books, 1972) predicted certain behaviors the world could expect from Der Feuhrer based upon his family life from early infancey onward.

This report kept secret for 25 years, is now available to the public. It is a rare document because of its correct predictions.

Brill's book, which deals with the lives of hard-core addicts, entitled "The De-Addiction Process" (Springfield, Mo.: Charles C. Thomas, 1972) also notes the heartbreaking relationship of the adolescent's negative behavior to his early childhood.

In other articles I have alluded to the fact that adoptive parents need to consider, if they are adopting children past the age of three, the emotional climate in which the child has had to live. Of more consequence is the singular importance all parents need to give to the manner in which they respond to their children, especially when the children are acting up.

I sat next to a very nice couple with four children the other day while we were waiting for a bus. I was literally astounded at the father's continual derisive, cruel and unusual short-temperedness with the next-to-youngest child...a boy, of course. The father, during a twenty minute period of time, shamed the child over and over and spatted him continually for behavior that was not in the least unusual for a tired and hungry six-year-old with nothing to do but wait.

Should this behavior be a regular part of the child's relationship to his father, I would venture to predict that the hostility and humiliation bred by this type of discipline would one day result in a vengeance upon these parents which would defy their understanding.

Children learn their aggressive behavior by modeling themselves after the significant adults in their lives. Harsh and threatening discipline teaches like behavior.

The children who do cruel things to animals and peers are often those who themselves have been the victims of cruel and unusual childhood experiences in chastisement.

Vincent Fontana's Somewhere a Child is Dying (New York: Macmillan, 1973) is the vivid account of the "maltreatment syndrome." Here the stories of children beaten by their parents show that these parents were themselves maltreated in childhood.

It is almost beyond belief to realize that some parents will single out a child to be the butt of their venomous hatred against their own parents.

I am the consultant to a Mother's Program in New York City which, on Ward's Island in New York, attempts to retrain female addicts who are mothers so that they might not bring up *their* children in the same mode.

Most of these addicts are the products of homes where they were horribly treated. They take their vengeance and anger out on their own children because that is all *they* have learned at home.

All families need to carefully assess their relationships to each of their children. Even "nice" families sometimes scapegoat, hurt, tear to shreds, both physically and psychologically, the children they say they love.

It isn't so much to protect the children that I make this call, but rather to protect the unborn generations who will, because of childhood abuse, teach their children to behave similarly.

If you are shredding your children with sarcasm, innuendo, aggressive physical behavior, you need to seek help before you guarantee your posterity more than its share of misery in childhood.

Child Abuse

Child abuse is the most common cause of death in children.

Parents who abuse their children are not all sadistic monsters. Most often they themselves have been maltreated and they learned this behavior when they were children.

Children brought up in homes where there is abuse grow into adults who are socially destructive and who translate their bad feelings into hostile and violent abuse upon their own children.

It is wrong to assume that they are vile creatures to be done away with for their cruelty. They are more than likely the products of violent homes.

As the world's stresses increase, whatever they may be, folks brought up on violence and maltreatment become even worse than their own parents.

Thus, in every sense of the word the homes where children are abused are virtually training arenas for the next generation of child abusers.

There are no simple solutions to this horrendous problem. It is clear that, no matter how personally affronted we are with people who abuse their children, merely putting these parents in jail is no solution at all.

Expert opinion holds that there are three things that need to be done:

1. Remove the child from the home speedily; and once it has been determined that there is willful abuse, do not return him until there is reasonable certainty that it is safe to do so.

2. Make sure the parents are undergoing treatment and are being taught how to parent, before the child is returned to them.

3. Reconstruct the family under surveillance and therapy so that any reconciliation can be effected under supervision.

I have already proposed to various state agencies that families involved in child abuse need to be temporarily placed in homes or apartments where (with their consent, if they want the child back) their 24-hour activities can be monitored.

Then, when crisis situations arise, professionals can help them on the spot with a type of intervention that will teach better parent/child relations under stress.

Jail never has been nor never will be the correct place for folks who first need a chance to pull themselves together.

There are some children who literally fight a life and death battle daily for their own safety. They can become little else than child abusers themselves as they mature and develop and start their own families.

Of utmost importance is that all social agencies which report actual or possible child abuse follow up on each case intensively, lest through their own failures the children continue to be subjected to violent lives.

Wife beating, alcoholism, drug abuse are all terrible to live with, but at least a wife can call the police, cry to her mother or girl friend, even fight back.

Little children under five who are abused have no one to turn to but the state and vigilant neighbors.

Nature and Nurture

Whenever there is a serious crime committed, especially of a spectacular and violent nature, a great deal of research is done on the life of the perpetrator.

Soon afterwards we are almost certain to learn that from childhood on there were clear signs of the person's violent nature.

Modern theory does more than suggest that it is parental influence alone which shaped the child into the offender he became. Indeed, it is undoubtedly true that the "bad seed" theory has validity.

Research verifies the fact that between children and parents there is a very reciprocal relationship.

In other words, parents do have profound effects upon the course of their children's development. It is also true that children have a definite effect upon their parents' course of development.

It is reasonable to assume that about 40 percent of a child's ways of behaving are hereditary in nature. But which 40 percent? The remaining 60 percent of our behavior is directly attributable to our growing-up experiences.

The point is that while it is not demonstrable that there is a 40 or 30 percent heredity factor, it is undoubtedly a fact that there is a genetic attribute to human growth and development.

But then where are we? Though we cannot tell exactly where that 40 percent influences life's course, there is still a 60 percent environmental factor that we can do something about.

Regardless of the nature-nurture split or percentage distribution, it makes sense to deal primarily with the observable. That is, if we rely upon the genetic explanation for erratic behavior, we are too likely to ascribe everything of a negative nature to ancestors—particularly the progenitors of our spouses.

It only makes sense to deal with what is tangible, evident.

Thus, a good share of the books that deal with children's problems do not talk about how to offset the influence of an errant great uncle's behavior, but rather how to identify and deal with children's behavior at the present time.

For one thing, overdependence upon ancestor-related cause of behavior places too great a burden upon our ancestors, who generally had very little to do with their genetic heritage. For another, it is a hopeless philosophy since it means that what is in the genes is not subject to amelioration.

The only thing nice that can be said about trying to trace our children's behavior to their heredity is that we are more likely to try to find the exemplary behavior that is attributable to "good old Uncle John way back when...."

But it is a "cop out" to turn from the actual solving of children's aberrant behavior, and instead, attribute it to sources, such as blood lines, over which you have no control.

When a Child Steals

It was a bright weekday afternoon. Marie was visiting her friend. The two 15-year-olds were very close and interdependent. It was routine for them to exchange T shirts, jeans...you name it.

In the same house that Marie was visiting there was a 13-year-old too, the sister of the friend. Marie dropped in for a friendly visit, spotted a gaily decorated, handsewn scarf ring and in a moment of temptation slipped it into her pocket.

Within a few days she realized that she had stolen. She had taken without permission from her friend's sister. Call it what you may, a rose by any other name.... In panic Marie told her mother the whole story.

What does she do next? She had never regarded herself as a thief. Indeed, one could hardly call her that despite the fact that she took what wasn't hers.

But how to cope with the emotional agony of trying to make restitution? What is the parental role once the deed has been made known to them?

There is only one correct principle. The parent at this point need not slay the child in anger, nor commit hari-kari out of deep shame.

Children at any age need to learn to cope with their errors as well as their successes. One act does not make a person a thief except for the moment of the act.

Helping children to cope in this instance demands that the parent enunciate the idea that the wrong and impulsive act must be set right, even at the expense of the child facing the music of embarrassment and temporary distrust.

It is now that the child learns the character of the adults who have obligated themselves to parenthood. It is here where the adult has the possibility of a shining hour.

To pass on a rich heritage of honesty is worth more than the temporary gain of ease and tranquility one might obtain from refusing to point the adolescent in the right direction.

Remember, the child has literally begged for guidance by disclosing the pilferage to the adult.

The child must learn to cope with her shame and chagrin. Adult dalliance only leads to deep feelings of disappointment in and for the parents who, ostrich-like, chose to make believe that nothing really happened that hadn't occurred before.

When children ask adults to help them sort out their world of right and wrong, to cope with circumstances which may well have momentarily overwhelmed them, it is the function of adults to shoot from the shoulder and help the children chart a course of responsible behavior.

Anything less shrivels the child's image of the parent and his own self-worth, and send the message that morality is only for certain times.

The Burden of Guilt

There are awful effects when children have feelings of guilt arising out of events they are unable to explain or explore.

For instance, a young man in his teens was a party to an automobile accident in which another adolescent was killed.

In another incident, a six-year-old girl was tending her toddler brother when he was run over by a large dump truck and killed.

In neither case was the surviving child to blame. The auto accident was adjudged to be the fault of neither driver. The six-year-old cannot be expected to be a responsible party in child-tending.

In fact, there are numerous cases of children drowning, or nearly so, in their own little tubs when the mother, running to answer a phone or doorbell, calls back to a six or seven-year-old to "Watch the baby. I'll be right back."

Nonetheless, especially in the latter instance, the death of a sibling can trigger an avalanche of bad feelings and guilt on the part of the remaining child.

He is liable to assume the guilt and shame for the event despite the fact that he is not responsible.

In one case, the remaining child was in his middle adolescence before the horrible feelings of guilt and remorse hit.

They came with such ferocity that 15 years later he was incapable of feeling at ease in his world, because of the persistent thoughts of the tragedy he barely recollected.

It is vital that such paralyzing fears be managed; that they do not cripple the survivor emotionally in his contacts with his peers and family.

Two things need to be done in both instances: Where an adolescent is implicated in the death of another, he should have the opportunity to talk out his feelings voluminously.

It will not suffice for friends or relatives to try to argue him out of his feelings.

It is the one who feels the guilt, who sleeps with it, who carries it with him, correctly or incorrectly, who must finally battle his way through the morass of terrorist emotions.

The feelings of guilt require a chance to ventilate the emotions. Time and talking will ordinarily ease the pain.

Next, where a child is involved in a tragedy he witnesses and where he may even think he is responsible, he too must be allowed to ventilate his fears and hurts.

He may need to talk and talk and cry. He may need to write of it, to draw pictures of it, to dream of it.

The worst thing adults can do in these cases is to gloss it over, to not allow an outpouring of emotions, or try to justify whatever happened.

Our feelings are facts to us. A child needs time and an opportunity to sort out these feelings, often alone—at other times, with those who love him.

The Family Connection

In order to understand why there is tumult and anxiety during adolescence, we need to realize that during this time in a child's life there is an almost continual search for connections—with peers, with community, with himself.

Sometimes this search becomes intense, even desperate.

It has been said that adolescence is a death and a rebirth experience. This is well said—for indeed, one dies as a child and is reborn as an adult.

For the first time in a child's life he begins to become more and more aware of his mortality and the possibility of his death. He becomes more willing to try everything and anything.

I know an adolescent who wanders the streets lost in thoughts of gurus and philosophies beyond his ken and who dreams of glory.

In a more extreme way than most of his peers he is, like Diogenes of old, searching for some connection between himself and things larger than he.

Well, you may argue, his family is surely greater than he is. Why doesn't he look for the family connection? He does. He searches with great avidity for some meaningful attachment to his family, but in that process of search he too often cannot see the forest for the trees.

His family is there and always has been. But perhaps the adage that "the intelligent disdain the obvious" applies.

The adolescent frequently becomes very critical of his family, and especially critical of his parents. Folks who do not understand this construe the hostility as a rejection of family values.

In a way it is. But it does not really spring from hate, but rather from intense efforts to find satisfactory connections which are, at one and the same time, independent of the family, yet not unrelated.

All adolescents, no matter how cocksure they seem, doubt that they can achieve this independence.

Adolescence is a terrible state of vulnerability.

The adolescent feels insecure and the less secure he is the more he needs to assert himself. So, he attacks his parents and family because he feels so inadequate in the task that lies before him.

There is a vicious circle bred. The adolescent needs to affirm his selfhood and vitality. He needs to attack what has been and what is, in order to be sure that he really has something to tilt against. Thus he finds parents and family readily available targets.

As he devalues his family he raises inner questions about his own biologically-mediated sense of connection. During the early and middle stages of adolescence this tension causes untold inner turmoil in his parents and in himself.

There must always be an element of tension in the relationship between generations. The wisdom of age is no longer a guarantee that adult decisions are infallible. In today's fast-paced, informative world there is less authenticity about age-related knowledge.

Most parents of adolescents are about 40 or so. They need to recognize their own middle-aged crisis, which is related to eventual death, keeping pace with co-workers who are younger, and the images of separation and disintegration which are becoming more and more real.

In a sense then, adolescents tantalize and antagonize parents with their youthful vitality and frivolity.

The family connection is the absolutely necessary ingredient in the successful transition from childhood to adulthood. If the connection gets "shorted" permanently, then the flowering of adulthood is permanently withered.

That there are "shorts" and "outages" which are temporary is good, expected, and likely to lead to better maturity in adulthood.

The family connection, to be therapeutic, needs constant repair, observation, and occasionally some binding with friction tape.

Youth Suicide—A Way Out

In 1950 the suicide rate for people age 20-24 was 8.1 per 100,000 people. In 1977 it had risen to 16.8. This figure is considerably above the average for the rest of the population.

What is it that makes young people blow out their brains (men favor this method) or take an overdose of pills (women try it this way)?

There isn't a simple answer. It would be nice to lay it at some convenient door, but the truth is that no one trend or person or event makes for this horrible statistic.

As man has spent endless years looking for the fountain of youth, youth for eons of time has been looking for fonts of wisdom which would reveal new truths and light to them.

It is in the nature of young people that they both reject and seek guidance from their elders. The various social revolutions we have experienced in this country have, at least since 1960, been attempts to discover new life-styles.

In the past few years I have talked with dozens of youths in various parts of the world who have gone into other streams, who have "done their thing." They have tried alternative paths and have made the discovery that their best remedy was to drop their buckets where they were and pull from within themselves the keys to the better life.

When young people discover that the keys to happiness have been within their reach all the time, it is often enough to drive them to the most extreme measures. Suicide is the easy way out of life.

Little wonder that it presents an attractive alternative to continuing the hassle with existence.

Studies of the street people, disappointed commune settlers, the hordes who invaded Berkeley, and others, suggest this.

The studies portray the shock many youths felt when the discovered alternative lifestyles were not what dreams promised.

So great was the shock that, all too often, Russian roulette provided the way out.

In Search of Love

Nell is 30 now—a grown woman who was adopted at the age of two-and-one-half by an affluent couple who thought it would be "nice" to have a family this way, since no other way was possible.

Only "mother" discovered too late (the year after the adoption became final) that rearing a child wasn't as glamorous as it seemed. So, Nell was "kept," but she knew she didn't belong and that basically a mistake had been made.

Just the other day she told me of her long and desperate search for her real mother and father. The story rivals fiction. At the age of 13 this child found in her adoptive father's drawer a letter which told her that she was born in Denver.

At 16 she ran away from home and landed in Denver. She made her way to the hall of records and there asked to see her birth certificate. Many years before, her adoptive parents had changed her original birth certificate to now read her new last name instead of her original name.

An unwary clerk pulled both certificates from the file and gave the child the original one. Even today her eyes sparkled as she told of how she saw her real name and how she vowed never to cease the search for those real, though unmarried biological parents.

It took four more years of telephone calls and letters for her to first locate her mother, now married and with four children. She tells of her phone call to announce to this stranger that she was in that very city eagerly waiting to meet her real mother.

Twenty years before in a moment of childish abandon, a pretty young nurse and a friendless, tired and lonely hospital aide conceived Nell. They never married each other and the child was born and immediately placed in foster care until the age of two-and-one-half. She was then placed for adoption with the affluent couple.

"My own mother screamed when she heard she had been found and told me to go away and not disturb the life she had made with a husband and four children. My own mother told me to go away and never come back," cried Nell.

A few months later she laboriously tracked down her "real" father in an Eastern metropolis. Her call to him resulted in mono-syllable words on the other end. "He never admitted he was my father. I was only a stranger to him," sobbed Nell. "My own father."

This crass rejection was more than Nell could survive. She started to drink, take drugs, and in general make every attempt to blot out her cruel past. She succeeded admirably.

Her search for love and acceptance, which she did not find in her adoptive home, led her into a very dangerous marriage. In less than a year it ended in a terrible divorce.

And here she is, 30 years old. No job, no future, no mother or father who really love her. The last 10 years have been torture for her. She has been in one institution after another, one psychiatrist's office after another.

Her lovely brown eyes met mine as she said, "I have found myself a little bit. I can now accept what happened. I even understand my mother and father even though they disappointed me terribly."

This story isn't new or original. What was once a night of passion for two "grownups" became a lifetime of misery for a little girl now grown into a woman.

Our acts, even as adolescents, are not solely ours. There is very little human behavior that doesn't affect the world around us.

This is the story of a paralyzed life which a dear child never asked for. Who says, who dares say, "I'll do what I want. It's my life, isn't it?"

Advice from a Convict

As a child, Charlie didn't spend more than a few months in school.

When he was 11, he dumped a dozen or so U.S. government barges over a waterfall.

At 12 he was in a jail full of town drunks and assorted woebegone men. One night, one of them assaulted him, and Charlie vowed that he would get even.

Released the next day, he studied the situation for a few days and plotted his revenge. He committed a minor theft, was imprisoned again with about the same men as before.

Awaking in the middle of the night he unscrewed the solid wooden bed post, made his way among the sleeping inmates, identified his attacker of some nights before, and then proceeded to beat the sleeping man to a pulp. His revenge was complete.

The next dozen years or so Charlie's life in prison was one long round of making very certain that everyone knew this kid wasn't to be fooled with. And they learned.

After spending most of his life in jail Charlie found Odyssey House, which usually treats drug addicts, not people with the severe, nearly psychotic personality Charlie possessed.

It took nearly five years of intensive therapy, work, a routine which demanded a complete change of attitude, the demonstration of cooperative and non-hostile behavior to make any difference to Charlie.

He left the program over and over. Gradually, although he was "failed" and "busted" from his various degrees of privilege, Charlie's aggressive, brutalizing behavior started to disappear.

Recently, he was our guest for dinner. He was an Odyssey House graduate. He was straight as an arrow. He spoke with an eloquence unmatched by any but the most competent, greatly experienced professionals in psychiatry.

What he told my children that night I used as the basis for my commencement address at a local high school.

This is what Charlie knows and believes about himself:

1. Yesterday is history. Today and tomorrow must not be clouded by yesterday.

2. When a person likes himself, he can only then begin to show affection and regard for others.

3. Because each of us is a part of this world we owe our fellow sojourners service.

4. Growing up can't be hurried.

5. All humans (in jail or out) have needs in common. Until those needs are reasonably well met, life is empty.

Charlie accompanied us after dinner to a local restaurant for dessert. A smart, street-wise policeman spotted Charlie for the jailbird he once was.

What he didn't know was that Charlie is well and alive and rid of nearly 20 years of misery.

I'd bet my life that no policeman will ever tangle with Charlie again.

7

Changes in Family Membership

On Newlyweds — First Problems

'Tis not alone the ceremony of marriage that makes a family. It involves more than signing papers. Any two people deciding to marry need both an emotional and an intellectual approach to their venture.

What do they face as they attempt to forge a family? The process of adjusting to each other's personalities has been more or less continuing during their courtship. But there are hundreds of mundane day-to-day routines which have to be organized. The challenge of establishing the daily routine, meeting mutual needs from showers to shoes, needs to be faced.

Everything he or she ever learned or did is likely to come into some degree of conflict with the other person.

Legendary stories about the differences in squeezing toothpaste tubes as the basis for separation are, at one and the same time, both true and untrue.

I have really never heard of a marriage that failed because of differences in the ordinary routines of life. I simply do not believe that folks divorce or separate because one or the other wears socks for more than one day or because one uses a water pik and the other doesn't.

What is true is that a vast amount of minor unhappiness can result from differences in standards regarding such mundane things as who gets up when and who gets to read the paper first.

In general, if there has not been a wide difference in the two social class statuses of the couple, the at-home personal and even private routines offer little problem, though they may be cause for adjustment now and again.

More difficult than the personal trivialities is the more complex problem of the newly formed couple separating from each family of origin.

Immediately after marriage there is the necessity of negotiating a different relationship with parents, siblings, in-laws and friends.

This very often is the first source of conflict as the new couple find that loyalties to their mothers and fathers need to shift to the new marriage.

Of great importance here is the ability of the parents of the couple to understand this shift in loyalty and not see it as an act of betrayal.

Some years ago I had a tearful bride call and say that on the morning after their wedding her husband's mother called and asked if he would run an errand for her. He dutifully acceded and thus began a running battle about primary loyalty which lasted for many years.

In the absence of an emergency there were three people who committed errors.

First, the mother, for daring to intrude in the new couple's life at such an inopportune moment. Second, the new husband who was not able to ascertain the difference between an unrighteous request and the honor he thought he owed his mother. Finally, the new bride who let him go.

Other things which must meet a just accommodation are the many extra-familial demands such as friends, work, duties and pleasures.

For example, a young lady came to her marriage counselor and reported that if her husband wasn't out with his old friends each night, the gang met in their new apartment.

In this case the husband merely added a wife to his old gang. He had not made an intellectual committment to his marriage. It is possible that he did not realize the nature of the new affiliation. Nobody told him his wife wasn't one of the gang.

On Newlyweds—That First Child

The birth of the first child can be a difficult challenge to a new family. The arrival of that newborn marks a radical change in the family organization.

Up to this point the couple have pretty much been concerned with one another. In fact, they have continued their courtship in a more relaxed and mature way, all the time learning how to accommodate for one another's differences in lifestyle.

Modern contraceptive technology has, in addition, probably prolonged the period between the marriage day and the birth of their first child. As such they have most likely spent a longer period of time with each other than was true in years past.

So, when junior finally arrives, he immediately is the cause of a certain degree of tension, mixed with the joys of parenthood.

Each spouse's function must be radically altered, with no time to make gradual accommodations for the new arrival. The baby game is for keeps. There is no giving the "merchandise" back if things get too hectic.

Whatever routines were learned in the years prior to the child's arrival need to be unlearned—presto! And we are creatures of habit.

For instance, the couple have by this time developed a set of sleep habits which have been fairly constant over the years. On the first night the new baby is home, everything that existed before is likely to be overturned.

The infant's needs for care and nurturance are something that no amount of preparation could make easier. You can't make believe you have a baby by setting the alarm clock every three quarters of an hour for a few weeks prior to birth. Thus, one of the most routinized activities, sleep, undergoes radical changes.

Probably, up until the arrival of the new baby the couple have been very attentive to one another. After all, for whatever number of years or months they were married there was no one else in their lives.

Between one day and the next a third party (or more) is on the scene and the entire quality of the spouses' previous relationship must change to provide the nurturance the newborn requires:

The patterns of communication and general living ways (known more scientifically as transactions') must change in order to make room, as it were, for the new baby.

Either of the parents unable to shift to make adjustments for the baby may enter into a crisis time.

An entirely new set of transactions must be established to supplant the older spouse-spouse relationship and to now include spouse-child-spouse.

Lastly, the relationships between old friends (couples or not!), in-laws, grandparents and the like need to be readjusted, since these are now cast in a different light.

That is, friends without children no longer share a vital community of interest and are likely to become less important. In-laws become more important now that they are grandparents.

Life for newlyweds is not all bliss. The continually shifting roles are a strain upon both the individuals and the couple's happiness.

Is Divorce the Answer?

Few marriages appear to be made in Heaven. There are, of course, some that approximate this perfection. For most, there is the usual and continual process of accommodation, compromise and empathetic understanding of one adult for another.

The proof of this statement is found in the very evident fact that people who divorce tend to divorce again. In other words, their dissatisfactions with their original spouses are still there the second time around.

Little is escaped when divorced people remarry. It is said by ancient sages, "When a divorced man marries a divorced woman, four go to bed."

Too often today marriages are built upon the idea that if it doesn't work out divorce is always possible. The Pepsi generation has infected even the elders. In California my sister knows of only one couple who are still married after 15 years.

In the last few years we have seen the rise of encounter groups, sensitivity training, transactional analysis and Gestalt therapy, to name a few. While none of these is designed to destroy marriage, out of these experiences there has too frequently arisen, on the part of one spouse or the other, the idea that, based upon their new acquired insights into human relationships, their marriage has been a monumental failure.

I am chagrined at the number of professionals who have "discovered" that their mates were less than they might be and who have shucked their commitments in the face of the revelations their various therapies have opened to them.

It would seem to me that when insight into a marriage condition has been gained that there would be an attempt to reconstruct that marriage based upon the therapeutic principles just learned.

It is not unusual for one or another of a couple to gain certain insights about varied types of philosophy, which seem to bear a particular relationship to them. An analogy is the recent discovery of the success of acupuncture. Few physicians will throw out modern therapeutics for acupuncture. What the wise man will do is to incorporate new knowledge and old and use the best of both.

Long before the advent of modern psychology scholars of human behavior opined, "Men should take care not to make women weep, for God counts their tears."

The callous throwing off of perfectly fine women (my experience indicates that sexism rears its ugly head here, because men seem to originate the dissolution of marriage, where "insight" has prevailed, far more frequently than women) for the "blessed" state of the single life, appears to me to be using new knowledge in an immature manner.

If a person were once good enough to share a home with, to bring children into the world, one would imagine that only the vilest of infractions would be grounds for separation.

That there is not the identical connubial bliss envisioned in the pages of Playboy in one's own marriage is surely not sufficient grounds for dismissal of a lifetime of association.

Who dares to play havoc with "humanistic" ideology by scrapping his own family for the incantations of omniscient gurus who have, oracular-like, opened up the windows of human understanding?

It is a perversion of a psychology of humanism to gain insight and not to share it, not to attempt to apply it therapeutically to one's own life.

To be very plain, it is a shame to take the fruits of learning and use them for immediate satisfactions.

There is an old Yiddish expression which has stood the test of time. It says, "Knowledge without 'saichel' (wisdom) is ignorance."

Let new knowledge be used to build the lives of other humans, not to destroy family.

More Than Room in the Inn

A little old lady I know once said, "If there is room in the heart, there is room in the home."

Every once in a while a family is faced with the decision about whether to share their family and home with relatives, friends, or children who are unable to live with their parents.

This has been the case with our family.

Living with other folks (and sharing bed, board and heart) is not easy under the best of circumstances. There come those times when, for example, both the child who must live away from her folks, and those who have provided refuge, question the sanity of their living arrangement.

At those times the family has to call a council, first with the principal immediate family members and then with the "guests," so that some arrangement can be made which will permit the relationship to continue or to dissolve it.

The easy way out of any business, living or marital relationship, is to end it.

The more mature way, and the way chosen by most folks, is to try to redefine the relationship and devise a sensible and fair definition of how each must behave in order to perpetuate that relationship.

It may perhaps be an old-fashioned notion the little old lady voiced when she opined that the heart will govern whether or not there is room for one more in any particular situation.

The mere act of accepting additional burdens (some may call it blessings, to be sure) is not sufficient to guarantee that joy will reign. All intimate living relationships take work.

Mere goodness will never take the place of intelligent, empathetic behavior. The road to you-know-where is paved with good intentions.

Even the saying of the ancients that, "Somehow, God willing, it will work out," is not a guarantee of success. People, even newlyweds, must consciously agree that wherever there are differences there must first be an attempt to talk about them.

Though it may be true that most men lead lives of quiet desperation, it is urgent that folks living in any cohabitative relationship learn how *not* to quietly endure.

The first step towards sharing a home with another (or others) may very well be a living attitude.

For there to be some duration to the relationship so that there is more than room in the "inn" requires communication and a firm understanding that when there is trouble no one walks around in silent gloom.

More Than Room in the Heart

"If there is room in the heart, there is room in the home."
If a family really wants to accept others into their home, then they can do so, no matter what the conditions are.

Even the economic demands of the situation can be resolved if they really feel they want to take another person in.

We have had this experience. In fact, we are still living with two adolescents in the home besides our own. When three 17-year-olds are under one roof, along with the rest of the family, it takes both heart and head to cope with the situation.

Even with a great deal of love in the heart, there are some rules that can make the experience somewhat more bearable for all.

Usually, children in a new home situation need a great deal more structure than most adults are willing to provide.

Structure comes from the necessity to develop a working system in the newly-conceived family. Everything from shower schedules to lunches needs to be discussed openly and frankly. Sometimes there must be a confrontation.

For example, if the new child takes a long shower and leaves no water for anyone else, the other youngsters have to learn to bring the matter up quite frankly and decide upon a way of operating the home so that no one is caught short.

Where the "new" child in the home has come from an environment which has been exceptionally permissive, it helps to say: "Your excuses do not constitute permission or approval."

So, if a child is instructed to be home at a certain time, and upon a very tardy arrival says that he was "busy doing homework in school," though that activity in school is commendable, it is an unacceptable excuse for not following instructions.

Many adolescents offer excuses for their behavior, feeling that the excuse, no matter how authentic, replaces the necessity for obeying prior instructions.

Where there is conflict between the standards of freedom which prevail in the "new" home and those the child has been used to, the only possible way of managing the discrepancy is to maintain that, "your freedom depends upon your behavior in the new environment."

A child needs to adjust to the new lifestyle, not have the lifestyle of the new family adjust to him. Trust comes slowly and must be earned.

Should the incoming child view his new home as a prison, a place where he is unduly restricted, it is then doubly important for the above statement to be emphasized. When the child conforms, he receives commensurate freedom. Freedom is an earned right.

It simply isn't enough to have "room in the heart;" some clear guidelines for behavior on the part of all concerned make emotions able to tolerate change.

In "Damn Yankees" there was a song that said, "You gotta have heart..." you also "gotta" have a head.

Living with a Foster Child

In our family, there are four children from two different mothers.

That always seemed to me to be a reasonably sufficient amount of people, in our particular circumstances.

Yet, when the phone rang and a voice, unknown to us, said there was a 15-year-old girl in Salt Lake City who needed a place to live because her folks were unable to provide for her, we included ourselves in the list of possible foster parents.

It's funny how things of the past suddenly loom large in the present. My mother was raised by folks who did not give birth to her. All of her brothers and sisters were raised in the Hebrew Orphan Asylum in New York City, because her Dad was blown to smithereens on the USS Tuscarora off the coast of Boston during World War I.

My first wife, who died in 1957, was raised by two maiden aunts who could not bear the thought of a child raised in an orphanage.

My present wife spent many of her formative teen years raised by a good family in Canada.

Without these gentle souls who took in outsiders, life might have been even sadder for all of these people.

So, the decision to be substitute parents for this girl was rather simple. The least we could do was to repay the world for the kindnesses of those who preceded us.

But children aren't particularly noted for their gratefulness. Children do not view the present with much perspective, and so our decision had to be brought before the family for some ratification.

There wasn't a single "No" vote. But there was anxiety. What would the presence of a "stranger" be like? Our child nearest the age of the one we were planning to have live with us seemed particularly ill at ease.

I have more than once protested that our family is not the ideal family in America. I have long noted that my wife and I have never claimed to be better parents than anyone else. Could this ordinary family, then, one even with its own problems, take on another person to share the burden of its sometimes tangled wires?

I shall never forget the day the child was brought to our home for a first interview.

She was beautiful. She was so alone, so sad. How could anyone not want her? How could her parents refuse to care? (Since that time, in April of 1974, we have met and wept with her father who cares very much, but because of circumstances is unable to provide a home.)

Every facet of your family life becomes subject to a tremendous scrutiny when the home adopts another. We wondered about our standards of discipline. We didn't know how far to go with demanding the same things we did from our own. We also knew that there was no agency to take her back since there wasn't one involved. We knew there would be some danger in bending over backwards to show our best foot only.

All of our fears dissolved very soon. No matter how hard you try, the folkways of your family life will persist even when there are strangers in your midst.

We did learn that there is always room for one more mouth, one more personality. We did learn that we weren't as bad as we thought we were, and that we had family strengths we didn't know of.

Best of all, we taught our children that, despite our fears, despite our general feelings of inadequacy as a foster family, that it can work, and that everyone can stretch his love a little bit more.

The Reconstituted Family— Memories

The most difficult kind of marriage is one which involves couples where one or both have been previously married and have children which they bring to the new union.

This is called the reconstituted family. There are the following three possibilities:

—1. A divorcee or widow with children marries a man without children.

—2. A woman without children marries a man with children.

—3. Both the man and woman have children from previous marriages. This is the oft-referred to "his," "hers," and "theirs" arrangement with respect to the children in the family.

One of the problems that exists in a reconstituted family is that the newly-formed couple have both been hurt by either death or divorce—and they enter the new marriage without the foggiest notion of the inherent problems.

There is no such thing as an absent spouse in the case of divorce or death. Lurking in the background of the widow's or widower's life is the memory of things past.

One woman told me that she could learn to adjust to almost anything mortal, but to attempt to deal with the ethereal shadow of another woman was out of her line of expertise.

When one marries a person who is recovering from the death of a spouse, there is always this third party living in the recesses of the house. This is to be expected.

It is impossible for a human to simply forget what was there for a certain period of time.

In any home the new spouse needs to have a reasonable share of authority, to feel that he or she is a part of the structure of the place.

There is bound to be trouble with a capital T if this feeling is destroyed—if he or she is compared to a former spouse or made to feel like an interloper upon the family structure.

In the case of divorce, the same shadowy competitor is part of the scene. Marital adjustments are nearly always difficult. Adding to the usual problems of newly-married folks is the feeling that, when divorce has been a factor, this next time around has to work. This puts an undue burden upon the marriage.

Where a reconstituted family resides in the same area as they did previously, there are all the complications of relatives and friends of both parties still rearing their heads.

Rarely can blended families just pack up and relocate and start anew. Indeed, there is some evidence that too many changes immediately after a traumatic event can further complicate life.

However, reconstituted families *can* be successful. If all parties are aware of some of the overt and subtle influences that may exist, then open communication can ensue and family success is more probable.

The Reconstituted Family— Children in the Middle

Jill's mother was divorced four years ago. She was awarded custody of three children. She has just remarried a man who was likewise divorced a little over a year ago.

His four children were awarded to his former spouse. He loves his children and he visits them quite regularly.

Jill's ex-husband loves his children and he actually likes to spend days with them in the same home he moved out of. And he has done this now for four years.

It is simple to see that the two divorced people who are now newly remarried are in no sense unconnected with the lives of their former spouses. For better or for worse, people once married do not wash each other out of their hair just because they remarry.

The true situation is this: A child, such as Jill, has a mother and a stepfather in one home and a father and a stepmother in another home.

Thus the child has four people tugging at her heart, her behavior and her intellect. It is entirely probable that she has four adults imposing demands, wishes and suggestions upon her. This is intolerable.

It is intolerable because there is every likelihood that there will be a great many conflicting pressures upon her. She may not be able to determine for herself (depending upon her age and maturity) to whom she must listen or respond.

Her new father has certain rights in his new marriage; her original mother is her legal guardian; her original father has a legal and moral jurisdiction when she is in his new home or even out of it, and his new wife, in her new home, has certain ethical and legal responsibilities towards the child.

Just suppose the divorce was not an especially amicable one. It may have been, in fact, bitter. Who does the child listen to? Who deserves more loyalty?

This is a problem that children cannot settle, using their own limited experience.

The answer to the problem lies in the concerned adults. It is they who must take some action so that the children involved in the separation do not live in a world where four or more adults are sending disparate messages.

It is the adults who must forget past differences and mutually[1] decide what is best for the children.

Virginia Satir in her excellent volume, People-making (Palo Alto: Science and Behavior Books, 1972.) tells this poignant story about a 16-year-old who was acting depressed:

"It developed that she lived with her mother and stepfather, went one weekend to her father and his fiancee, the next weekend with her father's previous wife and her new husband, the third weekend with her maternal grandparents, and the fourth weekend with her paternal grandparents. In each place she was asked what went on in other places...."

As Satir says, all of the adults concerned about this child were basically good folks who really liked the girl and wanted to help.

The horror of the situation was that the child was asked to take on the burdens of five different sets of people and handle their jealousies, hurts, rivalries and resentments. No child can do this.

In order to avoid this babble of confusion, the child should have only one set of directions, given by the parents she lives with most of the time.

The other couples involved should abide by these rules.

Children must not be made spies in the homes of divorced people or in homes that are intact. In both situations children cannot bear the brunt of lying and deception.

Adults can be open and honest and still not love one another. They become this way when they realize that their children must not take on their troubles. There can be no adult happiness when children pay the price for grownup folly.

No one will "win" his children by playing games of deceit with an alienated spouse. There always comes a time when the kids "wake up" and realize who the villain was.

---

1. In Joseph Goldstein, Anna Freud and Albert J. Solnit's volume, "Beyond the Best Interests of the Child," New York: The Free Press, 1973, p. 38, they advance the idea that, "Once it is determined who will be the custodial parent, it is that parent, not the court, who must decide under what conditions he or she wishes to raise the child."

Children and Remarriage

If the old quip that "at best marriage is difficult" is at all true, then the sequel, "remarriage is almost impossible," is even more true.

When there are children involved in remarriage, particularly where the woman has custody (and this is still the case in most divorce settlements), the woman may be in love with another man, but it isn't too likely that her children will easily dismiss their old dad just like that.

And should those children be adolescents (12 to 17) there is even less of a likelihood that they will find their mother's new partner anything but a shoddy substitute for their real father.

The anguished cries of mothers who have fallen in love again, only to discover that their children by a former marriage haven't, fills the air these days when there are so many divorces and so many more remarriages than was once thought "fittin."

Well, I haven't told you anything new. It is to be expected that children of remarriage will often hold a picture of their natural father that is, in fact, quite distorted.

He may have been every kind of a cad, miscreant or buffoon. But to his children who now face the smiles and clumsy attempts at fatherly affection of the man who has fallen in love with their mother, he appears as glorious as the angel that sat on the bed of Abou ben Adam.

It is expected that children do not necessarily fall in love with the men their mothers do. Indeed, adolescents faced with this not too unusual situation, often develop a healthy hostility to the "intruder."

A recent letter to me suggested in no faltering terms that a 16-year-old daughter was not only rejecting her mother's new husband but was threatening to doom the new union.

What may be done to bridge the gap between a mother's new love and the memory of father No. 1, whose effigy swings importantly between the hapless new husband and his new family?

Hopefully, much of this will be worked out in the courtship time when it is obvious that mom will want to reaffiliate.

There will be some hostility then, as a rule, but the more the children are encouraged to talk their disappointments out, the more they are heard regarding their hostility, the greater the chance that the new marriage can succeed.

What were once implacable foes of any man upon the scene, may one day become, at least, reasonable bystanders to their mother's happiness.

No one remarries for himself if there are children in the picture. They must be consulted, though not necessarily listened to. If the prospective couple realize the feelings aroused in "their" children the new relationship has a fighting chance.

In my opinion, if the deal is that the children of the "old" marriage must be shifted elsewhere (and I know a case in which this is part of the new arrangement) rather than live with the original parent and the new spouse, then this is a certain indication that someone is marrying the wrong person.

Anyone who marries a person with a child must pay the obvious consequence of sharing the new mate with his or her children. Anything less is blatantly unfair and even cruel to the children at whatever age.

Remarriage is good. It heals old wounds. Unfortunately, love does not solve all things. And so, clear and explicit understandings about the children of any previous marriage must be formulated.

Whoever enters into such a bond must understand that children are not automatically in love with their parent's suitor.

And there may be situations in which remarriage will hurt the children more than the separation in the first marriage.

Marrying a Widow with Children

The voice at the other end of the phone indicated a great deal of anxiety about an impending marriage. This young man was about to marry a young widow with three children.

Is it possible for him to find happiness in this new marriage, his first?

Can he become a real father to these children?

The answer to both questions is a vigorous "yes, but—." Happiness in marriage, whether with a previously married person or not, is attainable if everything in the "mix" is reasonable, and the two adults are willing to make it work.

Can a man become a real father to children who are not his? This is the more difficult question.

In the first place, the children must understand, from the first, that this stranger in their midst is not their real father. From a biological point of view, he is not and can never be.

However, the testimony of thousands of children so raised bears eloquent witness to the fact that biology,[1] though it may not be completely ignored, should not prevent a "new" father from developing intense, authentic relationships with his spouse's children.

The first danger is that the new wife, meaning to be loving and loyal to her new husband, may insist to her children that they call him "daddy." This is sheer folly and calculated to increase any hostility they alreay feel because he is taking their real dad's place.

It may be true that some of the children do not really remember their father. Nonetheless, dimmed memories may not diminish the desire to needle their new dad. Loyalty of children never comes from legal edicts.

The next danger in this case, particularly where the children in the new marriage are the mother's, is related to the matter of family discipline.

In this case the traditional authority of the father may have to be delayed until he has gained the confidence and love of these children.

However, merely because they are all occupying the same home there will be immediate opportunities for the "intruder" to require certain behaviors of the children as they share the new household. This will be the cause for some resistance from the children.

The first time the children tell their new dad that their mother calls the shots there will be a crisis. If mom completely backs father, she exacerbates the already tension-filled atmosphere.

So, new parents are always admonished to be aware of the fact that children, for a good long time, have a primary allegiance to their original parent.

The process of a division of authority between the parents is exactly that...a process. No marriage certificate automatically vests a new father or mother with power.

When the children in this type of arrangment feel affection towards their new parent, they will, of their own volition, be happy to respond to direction.

When children grow old enough to fully comprehend what happened to their first father, they begin to believe that the adult

---

1. It is possible, then, to become, if not the biological father, then the psychological father.

who nurtured them, who invested years of time and patience in their behalf, is their real father.

The shadowy presence of their original father recedes, reality is accepted and at the right time, their second father assumes his rightful place.

Meanwhile, the expected lament from second fathers waiting for the day when their "children" will honor and respect them is as old as this one: "If only God will provide until God provides..."

8

The Influence of Art

Going to Art for Authorization

What happens to children who are exposed to degrading 'art?' Films, for example, that are filled with smut, immorality, pain and degradation.

In answer to this, Dr. Margaret Mead said: "We are rearing a maimed generation. We are giving them prescriptions for murder, rape, and every imaginable form of cruelty.

"The people in these pictures have the outward appearance of their parents, relatives and teachers. They dress the same, drive the same cars—and the people on the screen seem to have the approval of the community.

"How can children distinguish? They are being maimed in their ability to empathize sympathetically, or face reality in themselves and others."

This "maimed generation" is daily performing vicious deeds. For example, in 1964 in New York City, 1,279 children under 16 were arrested for robbery, 131 for rape and 30 for murder.

Ten years later, the figures were: 4,449 for robbery, 181 for rape, 94 for murder.

While it is true that children have some normal streaks of cruelty, envy and the desire to be free of normal restraints, films that cater to these whims deliberately appeal to their lowest feelings and, of still greater importance, do not frown upon these horrendous acts.

Dr. Donald Barr, headmaster of the Dalton School, in 1967 said this:

"In the English classes here we study "Troilus and Cressida." Now, there's a vehicle filled with obscenity and violence. But Shakespeare's morality was conventional. While he is showing these things he also has commentators who stand by and say, "How revolting. This is no way for people to live."

Who in our society comments about the deadly baseness of what the children are seeing. For the most part, their parents see the same films a week later.

Certainly the adults in the audience do not protest. The spate of sexually explicit films, for example, do not purport to comment upon the immorality shown. Instead, they make it appear that what the children are seeing is commonplace.

To quote Dr. Barr further: "How can one regard the people who make these movies? I am almost prepared to believe it is deliberate—a form of satanism. A man who puts his pocketbook above the needs of his audience, especially the vulnerable children in his audience, is an immoralist."

What the world needs is more humanity, more empathy with the plight of any who are suffering.

Andre Gide once said: "People go to art for authorization."

Adolescents are vulnerable, especially vulnerable to any suggestions from an art form about their deep-seated anxieties in the area of sex and human relationships.

If the authorization they receive sends a distorted message, the children are encouraged to emulate those who send that message.

When children see movies glamorizing infidelity, ugly violence, brutality and perversion, they feel their sickest impulses are being authorized.

Dr. Barr concluded his remarks by saying: "I believe that nothing should be placed ahead of the psychological and moral health of the community. There is nothing which says an artist is exempt from the common conscience of mankind. People raising children today have enemies to fight such as they have never had before."

Juveniles Resort to Violence

The 1970s represent a time in the history of American films when that great art form has been desecrated by hucksters and demeaners of art.

Raw violence, sexual explicitness and inhumane relations between men and women have been exploited beyond reason.

I can already hear the voices of the avant-garde growling that I am, as usual, whistling in the dark and calling for suppression of "freedom."

I'd like to call their attention to an article published in the New York Times (January 19, 1975) called "They Think I Can Kill Because I'm 14," by Ted Morgan.

It is a case study of juveniles who are increasingly behaving in madly violent ways, so that police experts report they have never seen such mayhem and carnage in all their experience.

It tells about two youths, 14 and 15, who kidnapped two 10-year-old boys and subjected them to the worst tortures imaginable—setting fire to one, dangling the other out the window, pounding wedges of wood into their knuckles, etc.

And then they beat them so badly that a policeman said: "I have never seen anyone, not even a prizefighter, look like that."

According to the report, when they were through torturing the boys, they sodomized them.

Such a report offends, it stings, it hurts, because the innocent victims of this sick rampage could have been anyone's child.

It is my opinion that this behavior on the part of the attackers is learned. It has been taught by the cinema in an explicit, vulgar, unprecedented attack upon the sensibilities by adults who make money pandering to the basest in man.

In the New York Times of December 3, 1967, Joanne Stang asked in the title of her article, "Do Any Roads Lead Away from 'Rome'?"

Here is what she says about the films of the 60's when the present mania for violence and raw explicitness was only beginning:

"They arrive at your neighborhood movie houses in glorious technicolor, and are consumed by the children with the afternoon popcorn.

"They are not films which demonstrate compassion or love as most people know them.... What they feature are sequential arrangements of smut, usually completely superfluous to the plot."

And this was in 1967!

With few exceptions, not only is all of this true today, but is far worse.

Who speaks for the children of this nation? Who cares what weekly and oft'times daily drivel invades their sensibilities?

Teaching the Quality of Mercy

We spent a few days in Cedar City, Utah, at the remarkable Shakespeare Festival. Last year our children ages 13 and 15 so enjoyed watching and hearing the three plays that we decided to repeat the experience.

There were many pre-teens in evidence this year. I like this. Shakespeare is the last chance children may have to hear the English language at its finest.

Even if they don't understand too much, a little parental preparation at home (such as reading the plays together or at least discussing the event from an outline) can be very helpful.

There is one thing you cannot prepare your children for however. And that is the audience reaction as observed the night of the presentation of "The Merchant of Venice."

Briefly, the play deals with a number of typical Elizabethan themes.

One theme troubles me (as it might concern any parent who, in 1975, takes his child to see a play with anti-Semitic overtones).

Shylock, a money lender, lends money to a merchant whose ships are destroyed and who cannot repay the loan. The original terms of the bond or agreement were that if the money could not be repaid, Shylock could take "a pound of flesh" from the borrower.

When it is clear that the money cannot be repaid, Shylock insists upon cutting his pound of flesh. He is told that he may have his bond but that he must not shed one drop of blood. So, he is beaten at his own game.

Shylock denied mercy, and now is at the mercy of those to whom he denied it. If he cannot cut the flesh without spilling blood (as of course he cannot), then he is to forfeit his possessions and convert to Christianity.

Indeed, one of the characters, in an effort to show Shylock how unscrupulous and unmerciful he was, says, "Thou shalt see the difference of our spirits," meaning of course that there is a significant difference between one world's concept of mercy and the other man's harshness.

During Elizabethan times the enforced conversion of Shylock was seen only as true Gentile charity. One would expect the modern playgoer, however, to see it as cruelty and intolerance despite the earlier intractability of the money lender.

Yet, at this moment in the play, the audience that night audibly expressed their approval of the tables being turned.

My point: How does one teach children about the "quality of mercy" when the adult world seems clearly to approve of a judgment which is almost as unmerciful as the original demand for "a pound of flesh?"

I still think young people should see the play with their parents. During the preparatory period which I described earlier the question of mercy and justice might properly be discussed. Children learn manners, morals and justice from their elders.

As Hamlet once exclaimed, "The play's the thing in which we'll catch the conscience...." In this play we can rather easily examine our own set of values and perhaps teach our children the true meaning of charity.

Developing a Personal Code

My 18-year-old daughter went to see a movie the other night which was rated "R." I don't think this is the first time she has done so.

On other occasions I have written that after today's adolescent sees five or six years of American movies, regardless of ratings, he is likely to find that the ordinary husband-wife relationship, which most of us know, is going to be pretty humdrum.

Sexually speaking, at least, it seems rather apparent that the reality of movieland is far from what one will probably experience with one's spouse.

I don't even pretend to know how, after a few weeks of most movies, unmarried couples can carry on an ordinary healthy relationship which does not involve serious sex. The new morality is quite clearly part and parcel of the frankness engendered by the American screen.

The "happiness" of Hollywood love is pretty heady stuff for ordinary kids who don't look like Marilyn Monroe or Tony Curtis. The admonitions given me by my mother about how to treat dates seem pale and wan compared with the "quick moves" shown in living color in other than porno-flicks.

Anyway, my daughter came home insisting that I go with her the very next night to see the same film. And I did.

Prior to our going to the theater, she must have said at least 50 times that she wondered how I would react. Maybe she thought she should not have asked me. But she really wanted to know my reaction.

You see, the adolescent, by definition, is still very much the person in search of himself. Ordinarily he doesn't ask his elders to come along for the analysis. So when the opportunity presented itself, I took it. It is very important to me to study as carefully as I can the progress of my children's development, even at the risk of being seen in an "R" movie.

Just ahead of us at the box office there was a youngish couple who were going to the movie with five and eight-year-old children.

I could not believe that there are persons so callously willing to disregard a simple elementary principle. Any "R" film is either sexually explicit or filled with language no child ought to hear casually used—or both. This was no exception.

Surely, there can be no reason to expose children to either experience unnecessarily, even under the guise of giving them a liberating experience in language.

The movie was not sexually explicit at all. It was deliberately, verbally frank, and was filled with some of the most unnecessary violence I have seen in a long time, if ever. In many ways I was affronted by the necessity to witness both for nearly two hours.

It was of this that my child and I spoke. Without doubt this was what she thought. This was what she felt. But it isn't too cool for adolescents to say so before their peers.

This was her attempt to test her values against her parents' yardstick, and I presume to discover that we agreed on a number of points.

The confirmation of her musings, her doubts, her being able to distinguish between the trite and the excellent was a very important growing experience for her.

For the watchful father, it was further proof that despite outward rebellion about many conventional things, my girl had developed a clear code. And the code resembled mine.

I suppose that many fathers I know might have refused to go with their daughter to such a film.

You know, it isn't often that 18-year-olds let fathers into their lives. To refuse an offer such as this would have meant saying, "I reject your values, your thoughts and your attempt to discover who and what you really are."

Though I ordinarily would not choose to see this film, I am grateful that I saw it with my child, who in turn is grateful that she was a pretty good critic of the decent.

Community Responsibility 9

"*Yes, But Not in my Neighborhood*"

There is nothing more inhumane than having to live in an institution.

Be it hospital, mental institution, orphanage, detention center, no matter, anything outside of the family living experience is sheer misery.

Indeed, I have sometimes thought that committing a man to prison is the height of punishment not exceeded in its ferocity by flogging, solitary confinement or any other form of punishment.

Lest there be those who think that I don't believe in prisons, let me say forthrightly that for about five percent of men in prison there isn't any other substitute which will protect society.

The trend in the mental health and corrective field is to seek group homes where some 10 or 15 youngsters, patients or inmates can be housed, rather than the archaic way of herding hundreds, even thousands of patients (prisoners, detainees, whatever) together in an impersonal institution. [1]

But all is not well for those who have tried to find places for people other than in large institutions.

In Ossining, New York, last spring the famous Wiltwyck Home tried to open residence for eight 12- to 15-year-olds in that pleasant town. The community of more than 600 neighbors signed a petition and got an injunction to stop it.

---

1. In our Prentice-Hall text (1978), "The Exceptional Child Through Literature" (edited with S. Epstein and A. Stone), we make a more extensive commentary on institutions for the retarded.

In Valhalla, New York, the Jennie Clarkson Home for homeless girls tried to open a residence in a suburban neighborhood for 10 homeless girls. Eighty neighbors gathered to complain.

And in our own fair city of Salt Lake many of us watched as neighborhood after neighborhood objected to a group home being opened for emotionally disturbed folks.

My own experience in attempting to open up small homes for delinquent youth in other parts of this city were parallel to the two New York experiences cited.

Folks are afraid of people in trouble, and not without some reason. There are stereotypes that don't die easily involving juvenile delinquents, mental patients, orphans and even aging people.

It would be simple to find a home in some off-the-beaten-path community where there would be no one to complain.

But, for the fastest return of a patient to normal, what is needed is easy access to loved ones and the feeling that the outside world cares. Oh, it is easy to talk when the site for the planned group home is in someone else's neighborhood!

You may be interested to know that in Westchester, New York (about as exclusive a suburban area as you can find anywhere), real estate values did not fluctuate one iota after a group home was established.

The highest ethics and morality in any human situation occur when all of the folks involved are able to make judgments based not on their own little desires and needs, but rather on the broadest concepts of justice and humanitarianism.

It's funny, but what is often theoretically right becomes practically wrong to people when the house to be used for 10 alcoholics is just up the block, not in a faraway city.

It is up to every family to teach the real meaning of love and concern, by once in a lifetime (at least) sticking one's neck out just a bit.

Remember, the turtle only makes progress when he sticks his head out.

I Love You . . .

A recent experience I had with 110 teachers and 110 children was one of the most stimulating and satisfying experiences a college professor could have.

A group of Utah teachers from the Granite, Salt Lake and Jordan School districts met with my University staff, largely composed of recent graduates and some teachers.

The Oakdale Elementary School in the Jordan District was our home for three weeks as "Practicum '74" was in progress. The purpose of it all was to give experienced teachers the opportunity to study one of the methods of individualizing teaching—the interest center approach to education.

Each day was a full day of study, instruction and learning. It was a thoroughly practical experience, with real children, real teachers, a real school, and all the real problems any principal faces for 180 days of the year.

Fortunately, all I had to do was be a "principal" for nearly a month!

Each teacher taught just one child for the three-week period that the Practicum was held. Each teacher was simply told to "Take your child and live with him these next weeks. Teach him what he needs to know. Watch him carefully. Study what he says and does. Learn what you can about how he learns."

It proved to be a rewarding experience for all concerned. For instance, at the end of a day, one of the teachers stopped me to say: "I had such a wonderful day. As I finished working with my child, she turned and said 'I love you...' And you know, I have never been told that face to face by any child."

One day a teacher was absent. When a 6-year-old was told that his teacher would not be there, he said "That isn't so. My teacher will be here. She is here every day." When his teacher did not appear, the little one refused to look in the direction of his classroom teacher the rest of the day.

One ten-year-old said she would never forget a summer with her own teacher. Another said that having his very own teacher was the best thing that ever happened to him. It seems clear to me that children crave the undivided attention of their teachers, who must, of course, divide their attention.

It has long been my favorite saying that teachers have only one nervous system to give for their school board and when that is gone, there is no replacement. There is no teacher oversupply. There is only public unwillingness to put their money where their children are.

Between 6 and 16 our children spend 15,000 or more hours in school. How dare a concerned public support a war machine, and highways that destroy life (but comfortably take us to faraway places) while their children languish in classrooms where there are over 30 red-blooded active ingredients to one teacher!

When we really believe that our children are our most precious exports, imports and commodities, when we really feel *that* in our hearts, we will stop the nonsensical talk about paying too much for the education of children. We can't spend too much on them.

Most men in Utah spend more on sporting equipment than they ever do on taxes for their children's education. Come now, who is kidding whom? Are our kids only important when they are on the operating table or in the emergency room?

I call upon all decent men and women to demand fewer children per teacher. I call upon my university colleagues, wherever they may be, to help put an end to the folly of teacher quotas.

In an era where man has become more and more conscious of the need to humanize the human race, we need to insist that our children go to school in smaller groups.

The importance of children saying, "I love you" to teachers who really know them is a matter of high priority.

How long will the generations of children suffer under the myth that a one to 30 ratio of teachers to children represents a fair shake for the children?

Mormons and Non-Mormons

This is a very delicate topic. I'm not even sure I ought to approach it, but I shall.

In a recent letter to a Salt Lake newspaper a non-Mormon bade goodby to Zion (Salt Lake Valley). She alleged that whenever anything went wrong in her neighborhood it was her "gentile" child who bore the brunt of the neighborhood ire.

A few months ago a visitor to the area very directly informed me she was aghast that non-Mormon children too quickly develop feelings of inferiority and hate for their Mormon counterparts.

She felt, as I do, that if when growing up, a child feels "left out," "odd" and "peculiar," then it isn't long before he develops highly-aggressive and personally-destructive ways of behaving.

No child should grow up with feelings of hate for anyone, especially for those with whom he must share his schoolroom and neighborhood.

I want to talk to parents of both Mormon and non-Mormon persuasion and tell it as I know it to be.

First, one general rule of thumb which derives from much research into child behavior: The expressed attitudes of parents tend to get picked up by the children they are rearing.

The unexpressed or "covert" signals sent by parents are also relayed and picked up by the highly sensitive antennae of the children.

To non-Mormon parents: I shall not argue with your perceptions of what is or is not the attitudes of your Mormon neighbors, teachers or friends. Whatever your reactions are to your community will be mirrored in your children's views.

It is very unhealthy for children to hear from their parents that the world around them hates them and will do everything possible to degrade them.

It is most urgent that parents find in their communities the good side of the picture or at least that they, as parents, do not themselves feel unworthy and unwanted.

There is a world of difference between being different, from the first, and being despised because of that difference. What parents find in *their* world will become much of what children believe of *their* world.

To Mormon parents: Everything you have ever been taught has emphasized, too often in vain, that you love your neighbor. The assumption that non-Mormons, ipso facto, do not wish to associate with Mormons is unwarranted.

Especially where you outnumber non-Mormon neighbors, your children need to learn through your spoken and unspoken example that all human beings deserve affection and genuine concern.

All the church-going in the world will not guarantee anything. You must set an example, not just of tolerance, but love and esteem.

While mowing lawns on Sunday may irk you and the wafts of coffee aroma may tempt you, neither by deed or word of mouth should your children be taught that these things, in and of themselves, constitute anything but different standards.

Mormophobia (an abject fear of Mormons) is unbecoming in people who may pride themselves upon their intellectual awarenesses. Mormophobia is as anti-intellectual as race hatred. Anthropologists are supposed to study culture, not damn it or extol it.

Rearing sane and healthy children is very important. One needn't adopt or adapt one's neighbors' views about anything.

The obligation of parenthood is not to deceive children but to be so free of fear that even pious Saints will become only neighbors who are vastly different than yourselves.

Non-Mormons didn't intentionally grow up that way. They have as much right to their mortgages as Mormons have. No child should grow up thinking that folks who don't worship as they do are heathens who will surely go to hell.

Unfeigned love is a prerequisite in Mormon life. Wherever it does not reign supreme in your heart or in your behaviors you need to carefully examine your family and teach it the way to love and honor all the children of Creation.

Mass Busing

In the last ten years I have made many comments about the mass busing of students.

I have consistently advised that, despite the early Coleman report of 1966, which led the way in school desegregation, neither black or white families will benefit.

In the 60's there was some rationale for massive desegregation. Blacks needed to feel that someone, somewhere, felt their plight.

Even then most folks of either race knew that a court order didn't make for a more generalized morality.

Nonetheless, the law was needed to lead the way to a reasonable and just equalization of learning opportunity for the children living in the squalor of ghettos.

With respect to the schooling conditions of minority children in America, no one who has seen an inner city school can doubt that somewhere along the line since 1607 this nation did not live up to the New Testament's admonition in Matthew that we love our neighbor as ourselves.

In the 60's, as now, finger-pointing doesn't help.

In 1975 we were faced with nearly mass insurrection in Boston over the issue of busing. Coretta King, widow of Martin Luther King, herself said that "the futile shuffling of students from one school to another with scant prospect of a meaningful educational experience" is not the solution to the educational problems of black children.

I am impressed with the conclusions of two black women who have researched the history of desegregation and called busing "dangerously simplistic."

Biloine Young and Brace Bress recently urged educators to "free their thinking of the racist notion that there is something magical about whiteness—that without it a black or a red or a brown child cannot learn."

It is about time that Americans realize that quality education means equality in buildings, teachers and materials.

The answer is never busing, which seriously deflates a child's view of his own genetic heritage and sends him back to his family daily with the feeling that they have contributed nothing to his education.

It is nonsense to talk about travel time, lunch problems, fighting on the buses, etc. The real issue always has been that blacks and whites alike must build in their own communities a sense of industry and pride.

Each family must laboriously convince its young that goodness and strength are within them. It is in the slums and ghettos where the battle for self-image, worth and pride must be nourished.

Integration, then, is only one part of quality education, quality life. There is the indispensible necessity of the oppressed group using every one of its resources, both human and material, to send its own children the message of their worth.

When the spirit of brotherhood pervades the souls of all who live in a nation, then laws will be frosting. The nation needed Brown v. the Board of Education. But what followed in its wake has rocked the ship, not balanced it.

Epilogue

The experience of family is uniquely a human one. It is one of the most distinguishing traits of Homo sapiens. The duration of its continuity is not paralleled in any other species.

In the last few years the TV production of Alex Haley's book, *Roots,* has focused attention on the family as no other modern event has. The nationwide frenzy to establish one's roots (or at least to discover them) and trace them with reasonable accuracy has captivated the imagination of hundreds of thousands.

For most people the interest in their family genealogy has rather dramatically pointed to the notion that the family experience is at the heart of the human experience. Without the deep attachment to family humans find themselves rootless.

Another distinctively human urge is the necessity of establishing ties with other human beings who share a reservoir of similar ideals. While friendships often provide this, there is no place where the continuous sharing of ideals is so much a part of the everyday experience as within the family.

While it may indeed be true that as Thomas Wolfe said, "We can't go home again," it is also true that as folks grow older they yearn for the day's of yesterday when they shared childhood within the walls of their family. It is this phenomenon which brings us to the realization that we "missed" much of the essence of the family experience when we were children. And this is how it must be since the nuances of family dynamics is literally beyond the ken of the child. Yet, within our bones we feel, even as children, the grand alliance that is forged within the family.

For children, the concept of the family reunion is one of the great times to renew the play experience with the other children in the family. For adults, it is a time to feel the intricate web of relationships that has developed through the years. It is a time to feel one's place in the stream of family humanity. There are those present who preceded us, those who are our contemporaries and those who will follow us.

Despite the inability of children to fully conceptualize the nature of the family, it is urgent that family rituals and traditions be maintained and created nonetheless. The feeling of belonging to a family in the present, having the imminent possibility of one day creating a family of our own, does not escape the notice of children. They simply are not able to verbalize how inextricably bound they feel to both family future and family history.

131

One might even say that as children move into adolescence they seemingly cast off the family. In fact, they are so much a part of their peer group that for a limited period of time they develop a new "family." Whatever the biological family provided, the peer family does. And this the youth accepts, welcomes and even joins in a way that he never did his biological family.

Models of human growth and development (Erikson, Piaget, Kohlberg verify this transition of the young child and his deep involvement in his immediate family to the gradual separation from his family through his elementary school years. These models validate further that in the pubescent years (11-18) the young person often turns from his immediate family to an adopted peer group.

And then comes the moment of truth! The youth has tried on his peer group, often finds it wanting, is ready to start developing an intimate (marriage oriented) relationship with another person and suddenly he realizes the meaning of family. While its most mature realization must await further growth and development, there is, in the latter years of adolescence, the first glimmers of the youngster's return to the family fold.

The idea of family is far from dead in America. There is every evidence that the reports of its death were premature. Even totalitarian societies have recognized the impossibility of burying the concept of family.

So, up with family. Create your own family by adopting whatever correct principles you can. It is your conscious attention to these principles which will fashion your family. No one ever promised anyone a flower-strewn path. The family within your walls will reflect your hard work and devotion to the Ideal. Creating a family is worth every disappointment and frustration that must be part of the process. There are no instant jackpots. When, one day your children decide to rear their own family, you will know you were successful in inculcating the family ideal.

Bibliography

Anthony, E. James and Therese Benedek, *Parenthood: It's Psychology and Psychopathology,* Boston: Little-Brown, 1970.

Bettleheim, Bruno, *Children of the Dream,* New York: Macmillan Co., 1969.

Blum, Richard, *Horatio Alger's Children,* San Francisco: Jossey-Bass Publishers, 1972.

Bradbury, Ray, *I Sing the Body Electric,* Bantam Books, 1969.

Brazier, M.A.B., *Transaction of the Third Conference of the Josiah Macy, Jr. Foundation,* "The Central Nervous System and Behavior," 1960, Fremont-Smith.

Brill, Leon, *The De-Addiction Process,* Springfield, Mo., Charles C. Thomas, 1972.

Bronfenbrenner, Urie, *Two Worlds of Childhood: U.S. and U.S.S.R.,* New York: Russell Sage, 1970.

Bruch, Hilde, *Learning Psycho-Therapy,* Harvard University Press, 1974.

Fest, Joachim C., *The Face of the Third Reich: Portraits of the Nazi Leadership,* translated by Michael Bullock, Pantheon Press, 1970.

Fontana, Vincent, *Somewhere a Child is Dying,* New York: Macmillan, 1973.

Geber, Marcelle, *Journal of Social Psychology,* May, 1958. "The psycho-motor development of African children in the first year and the influence of maternal behavior."

Goldstein, Joseph, Anna Freud and Albert J. Solnit, *Beyond the Best Interests of the Child,* New York: The Free Press, 1973.

Langer, Walter, *The Mind of Adolph Hitler,* New York: Basic Books, 1972.

Lester, Julius, *Black Folk Tales,* Grove Publishing Co., 1970.

Menninger, Karl, *Whatever Became of Sin?,* New York: Hawthorne Books, 1973.

Monograph of the Society of Research in Child Development, 31, No. 3, Serial No. 105, 1966, "Adult Status of Children with Contrasting Life Experiences."

Rowland, Peter, *Children Apart,* New York: Pantheon Books, 1973.

Satir, Virginia, *People-Making,* Palo Alto: Science and Behavior Books, 1972.

Spiro, Melfor, *Children of the Kibbutz,* Cambridge: Harvard University Press, 1958.

Toynbee, Arnold, *Surviving the Future,* Oxford University Press, 1971.

Young, Brigham, "Journal of Discourses," Vol. 10, pp. 360-361.

Index